30 Days in Zechariah

An ordinary girl takes on an extraordinary book

Allison T. Cain

Many blessings,
Allison T. Cain

30 days in Zechariah

An Ordinary Girl takes on an
Extraordinary Book

Published 2013. All rights reserved.

Unless otherwise noted, Scripture quotations are from the Holy Bible, New International Version, copyright © 1973, 1978, 1984 by International Bible Society.

Scripture taken from the English Standard Version Study Bible, Copyright 2008 © by Good News Publishers.

Scripture taken from THE MESSAGE. Copyright © 1993, 1994, 1995, 1996, 2000, 2001, 2002. Used by permission of NavPress Publishing Group.

Allison Cain [atcain2@earthlink.net]

ISBN-978-1479307913
FIRST PRINTING

To order additional copies of this resource, visit www.allisonTcain.com
for store locations, www.amazon.com or
e-mail atcain2@earthlink.net.

Editor – Jennifer A. Strollo
Photographer – Sara Grow, Growphotography.com
Cover Art – Kent Swecker
Printed in the United States of America

*This book is dedicated to all the "prisoners of hope"
that surround me with prayer, encouragement and love.
Zechariah 9:11*

BEFORE you get started . . .

The book of Zechariah is an amazing, complicated, prophesy-filled book. There is a lot of controversy surrounding it and the meaning behind it. Commentators have different views, ideas and translations. There are just some things we will never know for sure this side of Heaven, but that doesn't mean we shouldn't dig in and try. We will work through this extraordinary book in 30 days, but we could spend 30 weeks on it. We'll cover the highlights, but there is so much more that we won't have time for. I encourage you to dig deeper on your own. Get out your study Bibles, commentaries, other Bible resources and take a closer look.

My prayer is that God opens our minds and hearts to receive His Word. These words that seem so old and were written so long ago are still relevant today. The ink is still wet! The words, visions and prophesies of Zechariah hold so much truth and relevancy for us today. May we soak it all in over the next 30 days, grow in our trust of Him and His plan and bask in His glory of His extraordinary ways.

With love,

Allison

DAY ONE

Zechariah the Book

Have you ever felt like giving up? Just throwing in the towel because nothing you were trying seemed to be making a difference. You didn't feel appreciated. You were discouraged and wondered how in the world God could do anything good with the situation you were facing.

Me too! And not just once in my life! That's why I found myself drawn to the book of Zechariah. Zechariah found an entire city of people who were discouraged and had almost given up entirely on God. He came to fill their minds and hearts with words of encouragement. He came to motivate them to complete a task. To continue looking towards God, to trust in His plan and promises.

I think the words Zechariah wrote so many years ago can do the same for us today. He showed the Israelites that God had been at work in their lives for years, even though they hadn't noticed. This is the heart of my ministry - encouraging all women to see God in the ordinary and another reason the book of Zechariah resonates in my heart. As we study this book together, I pray God will show you how He has been at work in your life even when you thought He had left your side.

Zechariah the Man

Although there are about 31 men in the Bible who had the name Zechariah[1], we are talking about the author of the book of Zechariah found in the Old Testament. Zechariah, the man, the prophet, who becomes the leader of restoring the nations of Israel. The Zechariah who received the word of God via an angel.

I felt like giving up when:

Zechariah's name means "Yahweh remembers".[2] You will begin to see how this name fits who Zechariah is and the mission the Lord gives him as we dig through the pages of this book.

Read Zechariah 1:1.

We discover right away that Zechariah is the member of a priestly family, but he was born in Babylon during the exile. He didn't return to Jerusalem until 538 B.C.[3]

Read Nehemiah 12:4.

What three names does it mention in verse 4?

_____, Ginnethon, Abijah

Iddo is one of the priests who returned with Zerubbabel (head of Judah during the first return to Jerusalem from Babylon). Who is his grandson according to Zechariah 1:1?

_____

When Zechariah returned to Jerusalem, many exiles made the trip home with him, but there were many who decided to stay in Babylon. Although they had been taken there as prisoners, after 70 years, it had become home. They were comfortable there, had made a new life and had grown accustomed to all Babylon had to offer. I get that. Why go back and start all over? Change can be hard. Have you ever had to make a change (either by choice or by circumstance)? Did it turn out to be harder or easier than you thought? Why? Write it out in the margin.

What I find interesting as I look back on my life is that the changes I chose to make have sometimes been more difficult than the ones I was forced to make by circumstance. I remember when I was working at a local university and a new boss was coming in. I didn't have a choice about that change and was anxious about it, but when it happened, it was a great thing. On the other hand, when my husband and I agreed we would downsize so he could start his own business, even though it was a change I chose to make, it was one of the most uncomfortable and difficult situations I have endured.

My thoughts on change:

What is Babylon? A great city of tremendous power and wealth. In 587 B. C. the Babylonians destroyed Jerusalem, captured the Isrealites and held them captive in Babylon for 70 years. (bible-history.com)

Read the complete story in 2 kings 25:1-25

The Israelite exiles were finally allowed to return to their homeland. They would be able to go back and rebuild the temple where they once worshiped and their families began. Some chose change and other didn't.

I have to admit I love adventure, but I wonder if I would have been too caught up with the creature comforts of Babylon to want to leave or if I would have been with the first group out of Babylon following Zerubbabel. After all, it had been like plucking someone out of a rural community and placing them in the middle of the Vegas Strip. I'm sure it was hard at first, but after 70 years the Israelite exiles became accustomed to all Babylon offered – good and bad. What do you think you would have chosen to do? Use the margin to write out some pros and cons of Babylon. Be honest and think about how you would have felt in the exiles' shoes.

As you can imagine, when the first group of exiles returned home they were excited. They were full of passion, vision and energy to start rebuilding the temple and the city their families had left so long ago. They started out strong. But, think of what they saw when they arrived in their homeland. It had been years since it was occupied. It was probably similar to walking into an old ghost town (just like the ones in old Western movies). Empty, broken down and overgrown. I remember when my husband and I tackled a kitchen renovation with a toddler and another one on the way. I was so excited! I could envision all the changes and the benefits. We started full steam ahead ripping out walls, ordering cabinets and picking paint colors.

But, (there is often a "but" isn't there?) as my stomach grew bigger, the house got dustier and the inspections took longer, I was frustrated. I became discouraged and wondered how in the world we would ever finish before our son arrived. This same thing happened to the exiles. Like many of us, when the going got tough and the obstacles began to mount, they became discouraged. I wonder if they all just threw up their hands one day and walked off the job site or if it was a gradual oppression that took them one by one until no one was left to continue.

The pros and cons of Babylon:

Pros:

Cons:

Fast forward, it had been 20 years since they had given up on rebuilding the temple. This is where Zechariah comes in! God sent him to light a fire in the heart of His people once again. To encourage them. To motivate them.

You will see how Zechariah shows his people that God was with them and was working in their lives – even though they hadn't noticed.

Are you experiencing a time where God's presence is strong or one where you feel God has left your side? Thank Him or pray He will make himself know to you again.

DAY TWO

Remember When?

Read Zechariah 1:1-6

In verse 1, it tells us when the word of the Lord came upon Zechariah.

In the _____ month in the

_____ year of King Darius.

This would have been October or November 520 B.C.[4]

When studying, a timeline or visual of when events occurred always helps me. As we encounter more dates throughout the study refer back to this timeline to see where the events fall in connection to the rebuilding of the temple and the return of the Lord's people to Jerusalem.[5]

So, things had settled down in the Persian Empire after a time of unrest. The hearts of God's people were being rekindled as they went about the task of rebuilding the temple.

586 BC
Fall of Jerusalem

538 BC
1st group of exiles return to Jerusalem & begin rebuilding

520-480 BC
Ministries of Haggai & Zechariah

520 BC
Book of Zechariah is written & Zechariah's 1st documented prophetic encounter (Zech 1)

519 BC
Zechariah's night of visions (Zech 1:7-6:15)

518 BC
Zechariah's 3rd documented prophetic encounter (Zech. 7)

515 BC
Temple is completed

458 BC
2nd return to Jerusalem under Ezra

Up until this point, Haggai was ministering to them. Haggai (who has his own book in the Bible), was another prophet and spokesman for God who set out to encourage those who had returned to Jerusalem to rebuild the temple.[6] If you take a close look at the time line you get a sneak peak at how the efforts of Haggai and Zechariah's ministries of encouragement had on the exiles . . . because it was only 5 years after they began that the temple was completed.

Read Ezra 6:14 in the margin and fill in the words below.

The elders of the Jews continued to build and _____ under the preaching of Haggai and Zechariah.

Let's discover how they made it happen.

Read Zechariah 1:2-6.

I love it when people get right to the point and that is certainly what the Lord did here. In verse 2 it says:

The Lord was

_____

_____ with your fathers.

Not just angry, but VERY angry. No beating around the bush here. No trying to guess what the Lord was trying to say. He makes it clear from the start.

Look at Jeremiah 2:5 in the margin. Why was the Lord angry with their fathers?

_____

In college, I placed God on a shelf for a while. It led to some bad decisions that hurt others and myself. It took me years to work through the shame and guilt of those actions. I have often wondered how God was feeling as He watched me fall prey to this world.

Have you ever strayed from the Lord? _____

Ezra 6:14 (ESV)
The elders of the Jews built and prospered through the prophesying of Haggai the prophet and Zechariah the son of Iddo. They finished their building by decree of the God of Israel and by decree of Cyrus and Darius and Artaxerxes king of Persia;

Jeremiah 2:5 (ESV)
What wrong did your fathers find in me that they went far from me, and went after worthlessness, and became worthless?

Have you let your heart get sucked into the idols of materialism, greed, lust, fear or anger? What is your idol? Does the thing that comes before God, rule your thoughts and emotions?

_____

Does it still have a hold on you? Or have you placed it at the foot of the cross? _____

Take a few minutes and in the space in the margin write out a prayer asking God to release you from the hold this idol has on you or thanking Him for already doing so.

What has given me peace over the years is learning through God's word that His promises are true. His love never fails and His mercies prevail. Look at Zechariah1:3. It says,

"Return to me, and I will _____ to _____"

This is God's way. When we find ourselves running away from Him or our faith and passion growing cold or our heart discouraged, what should we do? Return to Him! His formula for peace, joy and happiness hasn't changed.

"Don't be like your fathers" verse 4 says. Look up 2 Chronicles 36:15-16.

What did the fathers do to the prophets when they delivered God's message?

_____

The Lord is taking this opportunity to remind Zechariah of the past. How did it turn out for their fathers who didn't turn away from evil ways and listen to the Lord's plea to follow Him?

Look up Lamentations 2:17 and fill in the words.

God overthrew them without _____

and let the _____

gloat over them.

Heavenly Father,

Read Ezekiel 36:31 below.

Then you will remember your evil ways, and your deeds that were not good, and you will loathe yourselves for your iniquities and your abominations.

What two things will they remember?

_____

What two actions will they loathe?

_____

"So, in this eighth month, in the second year of Darius, the word of the Lord came to the prophet Zechariah, the son of Berechiah, son of Iddo." (Zechariah 1:1) reminding him of the Israelites' past, their sins and the price paid for their evil deeds.

Sometimes, in order to know where you are going . . . we have to be reminded of where we came from.

The influences on our lives go back further than we realize sometimes. Write out the names of your family members as far back as you can remember or knew them and put a cross by their name if they were a Christ follower.

DAY THREE

<u>Visions</u>

Read Zechariah 1:7 and fill in the words.

On the _____ day of the _____ month, which is the second year of Darius, the word of the Lord came to the prophet Zechariah.

Yes, again. This date would translate to February 15, 519 B.C. Work on the temple has been back in progress for about 5 months.[7] This would be a busy night for Zechariah because the next eight visions and one action item would all be revealed to him in one night. So as we continue, keep in mind that Zechariah 1:7 – 6:15 all occurs in one evening. It breaks down like this:

Eight Visions
1. A Horseman
2. Four Horns & a Craftsman
3. A Man with a Measuring Line
4. Joshua the High Priest
5. A Golden Lampstand
6. A Flying Scroll
7. A Woman in a Basket
8. Four Chariots
One Action Item
9. The Crown and the Temple

Have you ever had one of those nights where you felt as if you dreamed the entire night and never really slept? I wake up tired after nights like that. However, I bet after Zechariah's busy night, he awoke with a heart burning to share, with his fellow people, all the Lord had revealed to him through the angel. Can you imagine waking up after a night like that? Your head spinning with all the visions and predictions of the coming Christ. It blows my mind to even think about it.

1 out of 9 – The Horseman

Read Zechariah 1:8-17.

What was the part of this vision that stood out to you the most to you?

_____

I was intrigued by how many times Zechariah says, "the angel" who talked with me or stood by the myrtles. Count how many times, in just these 12 verses, Zechariah says, "the angel".

_____ times

I'm pretty sure that if I ever had an encounter with an angel I would say it over and over again too.

Did you notice what color the horse was that "a man" (v. 8) was riding on?

_____

Read Revelation 6:4 in the margin.

Revelation 6:4

Then another horse came out, a fiery red one. Its rider was given power to take peace from the earth and to make people kill each other. To him was given a large sword.

What was the color of the horse in this verse?

_____

The verse says that "the driver was given the

power to take _____ and he

carried a large _____."

Are you picturing it in your head like I am? Isn't the Word of God amazing?

As this vision continues, the angel reveals to Zechariah that "These are they whom the Lord has sent to patrol the earth." (v.10). I picture them as U.S. special operations officers who are sent into hostile territories to survey and collect data about a region of interest.

How does it make you feel to imagine the Lord has this army of special operations angels patrolling the earth?

_____

They report to the Lord after their patrol and ask the Lord how long he will continue to show Jerusalem no mercy. How long had the Lord been angry with Jerusalem? (v.12)

_____ years.

Don't you know Zechariah was on the edge of his seat waiting to hear the Lord's response to this one!

It would have been hard for me to keep my mouth shut. "Yes, Lord! How much longer?" I may have cried out. Well, maybe not in the midst of an angel, but I have certainly done that in my life. During certain trials or uncomfortable times of pruning, I have asked God, "Lord, how much longer must I endure this trial? Where are you in all of this? Please deliver me from this."

Have you ever had a moment when you asked God some of those same things? What was going on in your life during that time? Write it out in the margin.

The time(s) I wondered how much longer or cried out "Where are you God?" were when:

I never got an answer as quick as Zechariah did. For the Lord replied with (v.13) _____ and _____ words.

Imagine the relief on Zechariah's face when he heard gracious and comforting words coming from the Lord. I imagine it would be like my son and daughter, when I trick them by saying their names in a firm tone. They look up at me with the "Oh, no. What did I do?" look and then I tell them, "I love you to pieces." You see the anguish melt from their face instances and they reply, "Oh, Mommy!"

Look up the following verses and write out God's first response and then His final response. I'll give you an example.

Isaiah 47:6 <u>anger</u> vs. <u>mercy</u>

Isaiah 54:7 _____ vs. _____

Isaiah 54:8 _____ vs. _____

& _____

See also in Zechariah 1:16 where the Lord says,

"I have returned to Jerusalem with

_____."

God's initial reaction may be one of anger, but He never fails to come back with mercy, compassion and love.

Look up and write Jeremiah 29:11 in the margin.

The Lord goes on and explains to the angel and Zechariah that His cities will again "overflow with prosperity" (v. 17). Take a sneak peek at Zechariah 2:4 to get a glimpse of what this prosperity will look like.

It says, "there will be a multitude of

_____ and _____.

Write out
Jeremiah 29:11

Can you imagine the eyes of those Zechariah will tell of his visions from the Lord? Are you beginning to see how important Zechariah's ministry will be in motivating and encouraging the exiles, who returned home to a ghost town, to continue building?

There is nothing better than being able to see the ribbon of the finish line and the prize that waits to spur you on to the end and give you that second wind.

What do you feel the Lord is encouraging you to do today? What has He laid on your heart? Put in your path? In your life? What is it that you need a second wind to complete for the Lord? Is it a second wind to build up trust to make it through a difficult financial time? To build up your marriage that is on rocky ground? To build up what's left of a broken heart? To build up your faith and trust in the Lord?

Reread Jeremiah 29:11 and ask God to give you the strength, courage and wisdom it's going to take to complete your building.

God, I need strength, courage and wisdom to . . .

DAY FOUR

2 out of 9 – Four Horns and a Craftsman

Read Zechariah 1:18-21.

I picture the mess that these four horns (powers) created as they broke apart God's cities and scattered His people. Lovingly, the Lord sends His mighty craftsmen in to bring God's nations back together as He planned.

What did Zechariah see when he looked up? (v.18) _____ horns

These horns represented the powers that had scattered what three nations? (v.19)

_____, _____,

and _____

A craftsman is defined as "a creator of great skill in the manual arts; a creator, a person who grows or makes or invents things"[8]. In verse 21 the craftsmen show up. The angel reveals to Zechariah that they are going to fix the problem and carry out God's vision.

Read Zechariah 1:21 (below) from The Message translation.

I asked, "And what are these all about?" He said, "Since the 'horns' scattered Judah so badly that no one had any hope left, these blacksmiths have arrived to combat the horns. They'll dehorn the godless nations who used their horns to scatter Judah to the four winds."

Judah had no hope left and then God sends in the craftsmen to dehorn the nations that had scattered His people. What a victorious promise to end on today. How desperately Zechariah's people needed to hear this message of hope and victory.

Are you in a position where you have lost all hope? Do you need a promise of victory from the Lord? As we end today, meditate on the scriptures in the margin and spend some time talking with God about your situation.

DAY FIVE

3 out of 9 – The Man with a Measuring Line

One thing I am beginning to notice about Zechariah (even when he is in the presence of an angel) is that he isn't afraid to ask questions. All of these visions must have been confusing, especially with one coming after another, but Zechariah doesn't let that stop him.

"The Lord is my portion, says my soul, "therefore I will hope in him." Lamentations 3:24

Nothing clever, nothing conceived, nothing contrived, can get the better of GOD. Do your best, prepare for the worst – then trust GOD to bring victory. Proverbs 21:3-31 (MSG)

Write out another verse that brings you comfort below.

We see him ask several questions in Chapter 1:
"What are these, my Lord?" (v.9)
"What are these?" (v.19)
"What are these coming to do?" (v.21)

I do wonder if he sat up in bed the next morning, like I often do, and said, "I wish I had asked this. Why didn't I think of that last night? How could I have stood with an angel and forgotten to ask that?"

Today, we finally get into the second chapter of Zechariah, but keep in mind that even though we are moving along in chapters, this is all still in the same night for Zechariah.

Read Zechariah 2:1-13.

Did you notice another question? What does Zechariah ask in verse 2?

_____

_____

I'm so glad Zechariah asked these questions so we aren't left to interpret what it all meant!

Look up Ezekiel 40:3 and Revelation 11:1. What words do you see repeated that relate to verse Zechariah 2:1 that you just read?

_____

Why did the man in his vision need a measuring stick? He was going to measure the length the width of _____.

Look back at Zechariah 1:16 and fill in the missing words below.

". . . my house shall be built in it, and the

_____

shall be stretched out over Jerusalem."

Who needs city limits when the Lord has His men out measuring and has promised that the city will "again overflow with prosperity"? (Zech. 1:17)

The Lord is going to take this ghost town and fill it to overflowing with His people again. It's going to be so big and so prosperous they won't be able to have walls. I think Zechariah's mouth drops open here. I'm sure, even as a prophet and man of God, it is difficult to envision this desolate place, they returned home to, becoming a thriving city again. A city where the temple is completely restored and the people and livestock are overflowing. Everyone who stayed in Babylon will surely want to return home when they hear about this!

Look up Isaiah 4:5 and write it in the margin.

Isaiah 4:5

Then read verse Zechariah 2:5 again. What will the Lord be to His city?

A wall of _____ all around her.

I love this image. A wall of fire around His holy city and its people. God's people. I picture this same wall of fire around me and my family daily as we step out into this difficult world. Sinking into God's mighty promises of love and protection are what keep me going most days.

As the mountains surround Jerusalem, so the LORD surrounds his people, from this time forth and forevermore. Psalm 125:2

In the verse above, circle how long the Lord is going to surround His people.

The Lord surrounds His people for eternity; for always; forever; forevermore! As you read those words, what feelings start to bubble up in your heart? Make a list of some of the things you praise God for.

I bet Zechariah's heart was busting out of his chest. If it was anything like mine, it was so full of gratitude, awe, humility, thankfulness, praise and joy that there was no chance of keeping it all in.

Forevermore! What a beautiful word.

Father, I am so thankful for:

DAY SIX

Read Zechariah 2:6 again. What are the first two words?

_____

When my son was in Kindergarten and learning to read he began to pay close attention to punctuation. Unlike me, who over uses the exclamation point, he reserved it for times when he really wanted to make a point. He would say to me, "Mommy, this is the best day ever, exclamation point!" He wanted to make sure I got the point.

There is a lot of punctuation in the Bible. Commas, periods, parenthesis, etc. are everywhere, but you don't see an overuse of exclamation points. You only see them where the writer is trying to show his urgency or the importance of what is being spoken.

When I read that the Lord declared, "Up! Up! Flee from the land of the north" (v. 6) I certainly sense His urgency. The NLT translation says, "Come Away!" The HCSB translation says, "Get up!" and the KJ translations says, "Ho, ho" and the NIV says, "Come! Come!"

In other words GET UP AND COME HOME NOW! Get out of Babylon before I arrive to take care of these evil men.

In verse 7 you see it again, "Up! Escape to Zion, you who dwell with the daughter of Babylon." This is exactly what I do to my children when I mean business. When I want to make sure I have gotten my point across, I repeat myself. Sometimes, I even make them repeat it back to me so there is no room for the "but, I didn't hear you" argument.

Read Isaiah 52:11 in the margin and fill in the words on the following page.

> Depart, depart, go out from there! Touch no unclean thing! Come out from it and be pure, you who carry the articles of the LORD's house.
> Isaiah 52:11

"Depart, touch not _____ thing . . . .

_____
yourselves.

In these few verses, I see God turn a page on the life of these captives. He has returned, as promised, to protect them and avenge the evil that overtook them. The Message translation says this:

God-of-the-Angel-Armies, the One of Glory who sent me on my mission, commenting on the godless nations who stripped you and left you homeless, said, "Anyone who hits you, hits me—bloodies my nose, blackens my eye. Yes, and at the right time I'll give the signal and they'll be stripped and thrown out by their own servants." Then you'll know for sure that God-of-the-Angel-Armies sent me on this mission. Zechariah 2:8-9

I want to stand up in my seat right now and cheer. Praise God He takes it personally when someone trespasses against us - His children.

If you have your own children, you have probably felt this way too. When your son or daughter comes home from school or the park and shares how they were treated unfairly, teased or left out, you felt this way. Oh, yes! I admit it there have been a few times I had to pray for God not to allow my tongue to speak until I had my emotions under control. One thing we sometimes forget, in the heat of the moment, is that revenge is God's job – not ours.

Look at verse 12 and fill in the missing word below.

"And the Lord will inherit _____

as his portion in the holy land, and will

_____ choose Jerusalem.

Circle the word <u>portion</u> in the verse. The Lord was going to inherit Judah as His part, His asset, His piece, His share, His section of the Holy Land.

My thoughts and feelings after reading Zechariah 2:8-9.

After He declares His portion, verse 13 closes reminding them to "Be silent, all flesh, before the Lord, for he has roused himself from his holy dwelling." In other words, be quiet! Listen up for God. Be alert! God is on the move. Don't miss it!

I have goose bumps all down my back. What a glorious reminder that God is at work in our lives. Every single day. We may have grown numb to His touch, blind to His ways or hardened to His love, but He is still there. Still working. Still loving. Still seeking your heart.

Where is God moving in your life? Where have you sensed His nudge? His presence? Make a commitment today to be silent, to listen and to move at His request.

Write any thoughts, questions or prayers you have for God in the margin as we close today.

Thoughts ~

Questions ~

Prayers~

DAY SEVEN

4 out of 9 – Joshua

Read Zechariah 3. Don't worry. There are only ten verses. As you read it picture a courtroom with an angel presiding as the judge and Joshua as the defendant.

Who is the other character introduced in verse 1? _____

In Hebrew Satan means "adversary" and in the Greek it means "accuser". However, Messiah means "advocate".[9] And just as in a modern day courtroom, we read Satan (the prosecutor) is standing on the right side accusing Joshua, but accusing him of what? It's almost like Satan is teasing the Lord. Inquiring why His "chosen" people are so messed up. Let's face it. They had certainly seen better days when it came to spiritual or behavioral areas.

It may cross your mind, like it did mine, what are our Heavenly Father and His angels doing hanging out with Satan. Take a look at Job 2:1 in the margin.

The Sons of God and also _____ presented themselves to the Lord.

Although Satan had strayed from God, he was still a son of our Lord. So he showed up at heavenly meetings, not as an advocate, but a troublemaker. Strangely enough, Satan sits among the angels in Heaven on occasion. I wonder how that makes the angels feel? Are they used to it? Have they come to expect the accusations he makes about us to our Heavenly Father knowing Jesus will come to our defense? Advocating for us. Proclaiming we are marked by His blood. It makes me think about meetings, committees or even my own family. Usually, there is one person, who it seems, their one gift is to stir the pot. Anyone come to mind for you?

I love how the Lord responds to Satan. Fill in the blanks below. (v.2)

The Lord _____ you,

O Satan! The Lord who as chosen _____

rebuke you! Is not this a burning _____

_____ from the fire?"

I have typed out the definitions for two of the words you filled in above. Go back and reread the verse, replacing the word with its definition and see how it gives it a deeper meaning.

Rebuke - To criticize or reprove sharply; reprimand[10]

Pluck/Snatch - To remove or detach by grasping and pulling abruptly[11]

I love this! The Lord recognizes Jerusalem's sin to Satan. Probably says, "Look, Satan. My people have been in captivity for 70 years due to their unlawful ways, but it's time and I'm delivering them from the fire!"

On another day the angels came to present themselves before the LORD, and Satan also came with them to present himself before him.
Job 2:1

So the prosecutor and the defense have spoken and we find Joshua standing before the angel awaiting the verdict.

Joshua was clothed in _____ garments (v.3). Covered in the filth of sin. But, the angel says, "remove these filthy garments from him."(v. 4) Joshua was given new clothes and all his iniquity taken away. All of his wickedness, injustice and sin taken away.

I wonder how many times the Lord has had to defend me and my actions to Satan. It's embarrassing to think how great the number is. The wonderful news is that no matter how many times it has been, our Lord has plucked us from the fire, forgiven us and clothed us in His righteousness. Do you accept and believe that all of your past transgressions have been forgiven through repentance and the blood of the cross? Are there still some things you are holding onto in your heart? Things you think are way too horrible to be forgiven. Write them at the foot of the cross in the margin and pray that God will give you the courage and strength to accept that truth. The truth that you are a child of God and you are forgiven.

DAY EIGHT

Read Zechariah 3:7.

Then, the promise comes. " . . . If you will

_____

in my ways and keep my charge, then you shall rule my house (temple), have charge over my courts and access to those standing here."

Look up the following verses and write out what they must do to rule the Lord's house and keep His charge.

Joshua 1:7-9 (in the margin)

_____

_____

_____

_____

1 Kings 2:3

_____

_____

Ezekiel 44:6

_____

_____

Joshua, Jerusalem and its people are totally forgiven. They are washed clean from all sin, but aren't getting off without some directives. However, following God in all his ways, laws and commands is much better than 70 more years as captives!

Oh, and He saved the best for last. The last part of this vision is the greatest promise of them all.

In verse 8 it says,

"I will bring my _____, the

_____.

His servant! Read Isaiah 42:1.

Who will the Lord uphold, delight in and who will bring justice to the nations?

Who is His servant? _____

Read Isaiah 11:1 and Jeremiah 23:5 in the margin on the following page.

According to these verses, who is the Branch that God will send?

_____

Some commentators think the Branch Isaiah and Jeremiah are referring to could be Joshua, while others believe it's Jesus. I'm going with Jesus! So, right there in that courtroom before Satan and the angels we hear the Lord proclaiming – foretelling the coming of His Son, Jesus. The Messiah. The Advocate. The Savior.

The angel of the Lord continues. Write out Zechariah 3:9 in the margin.

Stick with me. This is worth it. I promise! Look up the following verses and write out the common theme.

Matthew 21:42
1 Corinthians 3:11
1 Peter 2:6

Common Theme:

_____

_____

There it is! Living with the Lord as our Rock! Our foundation! Our cornerstone! And it gets even better. Can you sense my excitement? This is the kind of thing that should bring us so much faith, trust, promise and peace that we are jumping out of our skin.

The stone with seven eyes, I know. I know. It sounds strange when you first read it, but look up Revelation 5:6. What do the seven eyes represent?

_____

Oh, how I love to know that our God has sent these seven spirits out all over the earth to keep a watchful eye on us.

In verse 9. How many days will it take for the Lord to remove its iniquity?

_____

Zechariah 3:9

A shoot will come up from the stump of Jesse; from his roots a Branch will bear fruit.
Isaiah 11:1

"The days are coming," declares the LORD," when I will raise up for David a righteous Branch, a King who will reign wisely and do what is just and right in the land.
Jeremiah 23:5

And after all of that, you will get to sit under "his vine and fig tree". Really, you might say. Gosh, thanks for nothing. Such an anticlimactic way to end such a marvelous vision, but the vine and fig tree symbolize prosperity and peace.

Do you have a place of security and peace? A place where you can go to be quiet with God? A place you can safely share your thoughts with the Lord and be at peace in the stillness?

Where is that place?

_____

If you don't have a place like that, make a list of some possible places that you could adopt as your fig tree in the margin.

Take this seriously. We all need a place we can get away from the world, recharge with God and seek His face through His written word. Make it a priority. The benefits are endless.

―――――――――――――

DAY NINE

5 out of 9 – The Golden Lampstand

Read Zechariah 4:1-14.

Sometimes, when I first read Biblical text, especially if it's ancestry, history or something else difficult to comprehend like visions and dreams, I zone out. Zechariah 4 did that to me, but when I slow down and take it verse by verse the scriptures begin to come alive, to make sense. So, hang in there with me while we work through the vision of the golden lampstand.

In verse 1, Zechariah makes it very clear that the angel woke him out of his sleep. I can hear him saying, "Let me be clear, people. It was a long night. . .

Possible meeting places and times with God:

I was exhausted from all the previous visions, the angel was keeping me busy, but I was awake!"

Even if he was tired and kept falling back asleep, this was important enough for an angel to keep nudging Zechariah awake. "Dude, wake up! What do you see?" he asks Zechariah in verse 2. (Ok, maybe he didn't call Zechariah "dude").

When Zechariah does wake up, he sees something interesting. Fill in the blanks below (v. 2-3).

A _____ of all gold

with a _____on the top of it,

and _____ lamps on it,

with _____ lips

on each of the lamps that are on top of it. And

there are two _____

trees by it, one on the right of the bowl and the

other on the left.

Reread that one more time and draw what you envision as you read it in the space below. Don't worry – this isn't an art class and there won't be any grades. Just draw out what you are imagining in your mind as you read verses 2-3.

We see lampstands throughout the Bible. They may also be called candlesticks or Menorahs. Look up Exodus 25:31.

Have you ever felt like God sent you a person, circumstance or message through His scriptures to answer a prayer or get you moving? What was going on in your life at that time and how did God get you to "wake up" to His call?

What are they to make out of gold?

_____

Commentators say the lampstand in verse 2-3 symbolized, "the bright shining testimony of the people of God, giving glory to their Heavenly Father. The repetition of the number seven and the fact that the lampstand was connected to living olive tress suggest the idea of completeness like we see in Exodus 25:31-40."[12]

The olive trees were significant because they provided the oil that kept the light burning in the lamp. Just like the Holy Spirit who supplies each of us with unending grace as He dwells within us.

Zechariah isn't sure what all this means. He didn't have the luxury of sitting down with 15 different Bible translations and commentaries to figure it all out. He had to rely on the angel. Ah, the good ol' days! The angel tells Zechariah this is a message for Zerubbabel, the governor of Jerusalem. A message of hope and a reminder that with God, anything is possible.

In verse 6 the angel explains that it will not be,

"by _____ or _____,

but by my _____.

This is an important reminder for the governor. Read Hosea 1:7 below. Circle how they will be saved and cross out how they will not be saved.

"But I will have mercy on the house of Judah, and I will save them by the LORD their God. I will not save them by bow or by sword or by war or by horses or by horsemen."

The Lord was promising to overcome any obstacles Zerubbabel and his men would face in rebuilding the temple. There would be no large mountains (obstacles) to conquer. God would take all the mountains and make them a plain.

"In the holy place there was no window or place to let in the light. It was lit from a glorious golden lampstand, which stood directly opposite the table on the south side in the Holy Place. Made from one piece of solid beaten gold it weighed about 43 kg. (over 100 lbs.). In Hebrew it is known as the 'menorah' and has developed into one of the most commonly used symbols of Judaism." (bible-history.com)

DAY TEN

Read Isaiah 40:4 below.

Every valley shall be lifted up, and every mountain and hill be made low; the uneven ground shall become level, and the rough places a plain.

How does it make you feel to know that our God desires to lift you up in every valley, turn your trials into treasures and smooth out all the rough patches you endure? When I read that promise, I feel empowered, courageous and thankful.

I have endured challenging times in my life. Made disappointing and destructive decisions. Walked away from God. Watched a friend die from cancer and leave behind two adopted boys and a husband. Been there to prepare and bury my friend's precious 8-year old. Through it all, I have promised myself and God that I will not let any of those lives, those mountains I climbed, or those times I weathered go to waste. I will see the good. I will cling to the truth. The truth that God worked and made those mountains climbable, those valleys shallow enough so I could climb out of the pit and those rough places in my heart smooth again. No, not overnight, but in time.

What have you endured? What mountain have you been climbing? What valley are you seeking refuge from?

Do you trust that He will conquer? He will make the way for your healing and restoration? In the margin, write out a prayer asking God to reveal himself to you through your situation.

As the angel continues, we see that Zechariah 4:9 says:
"The hands of Zerubbabel have laid the

Heavenly Father,

_____ of this house;

his hands shall also _____ it."

Can you imagine how awesome it must have been for Zechariah to see into the future like that? I consider all he had worked for to encourage and build up the exiles so they would continue the rebuilding of the temple. It had been years since the first exiles returned to Jerusalem and they were still waiting for the temple to be completed. Standing there, Zechariah gets the inside scoop. "Don't worry! You will rejoice and see Zerubbabel complete the temple."

Read Ezra 6:15 in the margin. When was the temple completed?

_____

This vision closes with the seven eyes of the Lord keeping an eye on the whole earth, but Zechariah doesn't let that stop him from throwing out another question.

What does he ask in verse 11?

_____

What does he ask in verse 12?

_____

In Zechariah's vision, the two olive trees symbolize two anointed ones. In Hebrew "anointed ones" (yitshâr) means "sons of new oil"[13] There are varying opinions as to who the anointed ones are. Some say it's Zerubbabel and Joshua. Others say it's Zechariah and Haggai.

I don't want to get caught up in the he said – she said. The bottom line is that the two anointed ones will see the temple completed and worship in it.[14]
How beautiful to imagine that, like the olive branches that provide fuel to light the lampstand, so the Lord offers us an endless source of light and fuel through His Holy Spirit that dwells in

Ezra 6:15 NIV
The temple was completed on the third day of the month Adar, in the sixth year of the reign of King Darius.

each of us. An endless source of peace, security, love, forgiveness, grace and mercy that will ultimately lead to eternal life. Is your heart fired up?

DAY ELEVEN

<u>6 out of 9 – Flying Scroll</u>

Read Zechariah 5:1-4.

Short and sweet. Well, not so sweet for those who don't follow God's laws because all they have to look forward to is being destroyed and banished. Yikes!

Zechariah sees a scroll flying through the air. If you are like me, you picture a small scroll. One you may see in Jewish synagogues or museums, but this was no ordinary scroll because we don't serve an ordinary God!
Verse 2 tells us that the scroll is 20 cubits by 10 cubits. In measurement standards today this would be 30 feet long and 15 feet wide.

Read 1 Kings 6:3 in the margin. Do you see anything interesting?

This measurement (20 cubits X 10 cubits) was also significant because they were the same dimensions of the temple porch where the laws of God were usually read.[15] Don't you just love how God weaves it all together and never skips a detail?

My husband is great at visual measurements. He can walk in a room and tell me it's 12 x 12, but I do not have that gift. Since you have probably never stood on or seen a temple porch, imagine an average billboard you see as you ride down the road. That is about the size of this scroll. Only this one isn't stationary – it's flying. Unrolled with writing so that the Zechariah can see the curse that is written on it.

1 Kings 6:3
The portico at the front of the main hall of the temple extended the width of the temple, that is twenty cubits, and projected ten cubits from the front of the temple.

Galations 3:10
For all who rely on the works of the law are under a curse, as it is written: "Cursed is everyone who does not continue to do everything written in the Book of the Law."

Read Galatians 3:10 from the previous page. It tells us who will be cursed.

"Cursed is everyone who does not

_____

_____"

The angel doesn't list out every single one of God's laws, but maybe they were written out on the other side of the scroll just like they were on Moses' tablets of the Ten Commandments. Imagine two lists, curses on one side and the laws on the other. We can't be sure, but the angel does reference stealing and swearing falsely as examples of God's laws.

Take a look back at Exodus and write out the commandments from the following verses in the margin.

Sometimes, I wish God still sent flying scrolls when we needed a visual reminder of His laws while facing trials or temptations. Let's face it, every day on this planet and this world is just one temptation after another.

Write out
Exodus 20:7

Write out
Exodus 20:15

DAY TWELVE

<u>7 out of 9 – A Woman in a Basket</u>

Chapter 5 continues with vision number seven. This is one of my favorites. It reminds me of one of God's greatest powers. Read Zechariah 5:5-11.

An interesting side note:
Basket in Hebrew is *ephah*. It's a term used for measurement and equals roughly three-fifths of a bushel.[16] If you do a search throughout your Bible, you will see it used over and over again from Genesis to Amos as a standard form of Hebrew measurement. Understanding this will help us visualize what Zechariah was seeing.

Let's pull a few key points out of this segment of scripture before we go further.

The basket (v. 6) represents the

_____ of all the land.

The woman (v. 8) represents

_____.

The lid that covered the basket was made of

_____.

Two woman with wings (v. 9) _____
the basket.

They were taking the basket (v. 11)

to the Land of_____.

Have you ever been in one of those situations
that require a lot of extra grace, where you are
tempted to gossip, tempted to push the
boundaries of what's appropriate? After they are
over, do you look back and think "Boy, I messed
that one up!" or "I missed that opportunity to let
God's light shine."

Wickedness and sin can creep up quickly if we
aren't staying alert to Satan's tricks and lies. I
seem to find myself in situations like this more
often than I would like. I see it with my kids too.
My son gets so angry with his sister he just
can't help but walk past her and punch her in
the arm. "You are letting the Devil win!" I'll tell
him.
In Zechariah's vision, the woman/wickedness is
covered with a leaden weight. Lead is heavy,
hard to move. God knows we need a heavy
hand to keep the wickedness of this world from
penetrating our hearts and seeping out in our
actions. Although, that wickedness may try to
sneak out and rear its ugly head every now and
then, it's under God's authority. With Him, we
have the power to put the leaden weight on and
contain it. We have the power to send it off with
His heavenly angels to the Land of Shinar
(Babylon)[17] where it will no longer be a source
of conflict for us. However, until the day He
returns we must battle it daily.

I really lean on God when:

Look up the following verses. What is the reoccurring statement in them?

Luke 12:1
Luke 12:15
1 Corinthians 16:13
2 Peter 3:17

_____!

This vision offered Zechariah hope that the Lord would overcome the wicked and cast them out of Judeah so they would no longer be able to make trouble for His people. It offers us that same hope and promise.

Is there something on your mind or heart that you are battling? An addiction, sin, emotion or idol that you need God to take away in a leaden covered basket? As we close today, take some time in the space on the right and write out some things that need God to remove from your heart so that you can draw closer to your Heavenly Father.

DAY THIRTEEN

8 out of 9 – Four Chariots

Read Zechariah 6:1-8 and complete the chart, as much as you can, using verses 2 and 6.

Horses	Direction they were sent
Black & White	
Dappled	
Red	

Sometimes breaking down the information from a passage into a chart helps dissect the information. All these visions and angels are difficult to keep up with so it's good to use all the tools we can.

The job of these chariots was to _____ (v. 7) the earth, but before they went they would present themselves to the _____ (v. 5).

Heavenly Father,

What an awesome image. Can you envision our Lord, sending off His angels into battle for us? Where did red horses go? Zechariah either didn't include that or the messenger didn't tell him. Maybe he forgot. In the Bible, red symbolizes war, carnage, destruction and bloodshed[18] so maybe it had to be kept secret for other reasons. What do you think? Don't skip this one. Sit on it and let your imagination run. If you were writing a Bible commentary what would your thoughts be? Write them in the margin.

Look at your chart. How many colors of horses are going north? _____ (this is clearer in the ESV Bible translation)

What color were the horses? _____ and _____

God knew the North, which included Babylon, Assyria and Persia would need to have additional patrolling because Judah's main enemies were from these territories.[19]
So the north got two sets of horses – the white and the black. White symbolizes joy and victory while black symbolizes sorrow and famine.[20]
Those are quite the opposite so the balance needed to be perfect. What an awesome God we serve. He is in every detail and has every angle covered. The best war strategist ever!

And I love how this vision comes to a close. His

strong horses were _____

to go and patrol the earth. (v.7)

How does it make you feel to read that God's army was impatient to go patrol the earth and protect God's people? To protect us. Read how God's spirit feels in verse 8 and fill in the blank below.

"Behold, those who go toward the North Country

have set my Spirit _____

in the north country"

I think God sent the red horses because...

God's spirit was "at rest" knowing His plan was complete for His people. Look up Deuteronomy 12:10.

"He will give you _____

from your enemies, so that you live in

_____."

Our Heavenly Father wants the same for us. He desires to give us rest from our enemies. Do you feel like you have some enemies? _____

Don't answer too quickly. There are many of us who don't run from a human enemy, no one is chasing us down with a knife or trying to end our career with lies. Consider this . . . maybe it's not a person, but a nagging feeling of anger, guilt, shame or hate. Our enemies don't always look like the ones in the movies or the old western shows.

For we do not wrestle against flesh and blood, but against the rulers, against the authorities, against the cosmic powers over this present darkness, against the spiritual forces of evil in the heavenly places. Ephesians 6:12

God wants to conquer and give us rest from the enemies of our body, mind and spirit. How do we know for sure? He tells us!

Look up and write out the verses in the margin. It is just one of His mighty promises He offers to all His believers. AMEN!

Write out
Psalm 22:8

Write out
2 Corinthians 12:9

Write out
Psalm 138:7-8

DAY FOURTEEN

Action Item – Crown and Temple

Read Zechariah 6:9-15.

Once again, Zechariah "lifted his eyes and saw" (v.9). No matter how many times I read it, I can't fathom what it must have been like for Zechariah to look up and see these visions and declarations from the Lord. What an honor to be in the presence of angels and God's glory. I have to admit that even though it comes with a great responsibility – I'm a little jealous.

Here we see Zechariah get a direct task to complete for the Lord. It's very specific.

Write out the names of the three exiles that the gold and silver for the crown is to come from.

_____

_____

_____

These names are repeated twice in this passage of scripture. When things are repeated, that is always a good indicator that it's important. Just like when I give my children instructions about a chore or task they need to complete – I rarely (OK, never) tell them just once and send them off to do it. I always repeat it to make certain they heard me and understand.

As I dug a little deeper, I found that Heldai means "robust", Tobijah means "the goodness of God" and Jedaiah means "God knows."[21] How fitting. Just as we talked about before, God is in every detail. Right down to our names!

Continuing on with names and symbolism . . . Whose head are they to place the crown?

_____

"Behold the man whose name is the

_____: for he will branch out from his place, and he shall build the temple of the Lord." (v. 12) Joshua will be anointed by the Lord and the Lord will help Joshua complete the building of the temple.

Where have you seen God at work in the details of your life lately?

If you can't think of an answer, pray God will heighten your awareness of Him in your daily life.

He is there!

Read the following verses and write down the common theme from all of them.

Zechariah 3:8   Common Theme:
Isaiah 4:2
Jeremiah 33:15   _____

This "Branch" will build the temple of the Lord. This is it! The promise Zechariah's people had all needed and waited to hear. A promise from the Lord that the temple will be rebuilt by Joshua and Zerubbabel. No matter what obstacles they face, or enemies that try to overtake them, the Lord will "sit and rule on his throne" in their nation once again. (v.13)

Surely, Zechariah was busting at the seams with excitement. The angel continued and promised that those who were far off, maybe meaning those still in exile or those who would come from future generations[22], would return to help build the temple. He promised a plan, a leader, and labor, BUT . . . .

Only "if you will diligently _____ (v.15) the voice of the Lord your God."

Obey the voice of the Lord. How many times have we missed His whisper because our minds were too cluttered with daily life, the world, and other "important" things? How many times have we heard His whisper and sensed Him tugging at our heart only to ignore it because it was inconvenient or scary?

In the margin, write about one of those times in your life and confess your disobedience to Him. You will not be alone in this activity. I'm sure I could fill up a notebook if I had the time.

DAY FIFTHTEEN

Zechariah 7 – From Fasts to Feasts
Ah, a new year with new visions! As you will recall, the eight visions and one action item we just finished studying were all revealed to

Father, forgive me. I missed or ignored your whisper when:

Zechariah on the night of February 15, 519 B.C. Hard to imagine Zechariah had to process all of that in one night and it took us days of study.

In Zechariah 7, we jump from 519 BC to 518 BC.[23] We are in the fourth year of King Darius and if you look back at the timeline you will see this is after the ceremony to complete the construction of the temple, but before the construction is complete.

Read Zechariah 7:1-14.

In verse 2, the people of Bethel had sent their representatives to "entreat" the favor of the Lord.

en·treat means to plead or beg desperately for something over and over again. To implore.[24]

Simply, they went to plead for the favor of the Lord. What was it they desired to know? Look at verse 3 below and underline the two things they wanted to know if they should do. Then circle the month they refer to.

"Should I mourn and fast in the fifth month, as I have done for so many years?"

Seventy years earlier, God's temple had been burned in the fifth month by King Nebuchadnezzar as he tore down the walls around Jerusalem. Read Jeremiah 52:12-14 in the margin. That is why for the past 70 years they mourned and fasted in the fifth month. They were mourning the destruction of God's temple, but things had changed now. God's people had returned home and the temple was being rebuilt. So, it seemed like a logical question; were they to stop this tradition of mourning and fasting in the fifth month or were they to continue? I remember so many Christmas traditions we shared as a family when my grandparents were alive. However, after they both died our family floundered and struggled with what our new traditions would look like. For our family, it had only been about 25 years of tradition (not 70), but it was what we had always known and the transition was hard.

[12] On the tenth day of the fifth month, in the nineteenth year of Nebuchadnezzar king of Babylon, Nebuzaradan commander of the imperial guard, who served the king of Babylon, came to Jerusalem. [13] He set fire to the temple of the LORD, the royal palace and all the houses of Jerusalem. Every important building he burned down. [14] The whole Babylonian army, under the commander of the imperial guard, broke down all the walls around Jerusalem.

Jeremiah 52:12-14

There was much debate on when, where and how our holidays would look like now that we wouldn't be going to our grandparent's home for special events and we didn't even have to consult any priests – just each other.

Honestly, these priests were in a tough situation. A lot tougher than deciding where a family should have its turkey dinner and open presents, these priests had to decide whether or not to continue a long standing religious holiday. That's where Zechariah comes in and saves the day. Well, Zechariah and the Lord of hosts.

Look at verse 4. "Then the word of the Lord of hosts came to him." Praise God someone is listening to His whisper! Can you imagine if Zechariah had not had his listening ears on?

Read the Lord's response in Zechariah 7:5-7 again below. From the Message translation.

God-of-the-Angel-Armies gave me this Message for them, for all the people and for the priests: "When you held days of fasting every fifth and seventh month all these seventy years, were you doing it for me? And when you held feasts, was that for me? Hardly. You're interested in religion, I'm interested in people.

"There's nothing new to say on the subject. Don't you still have the message of the earlier prophets from the time when Jerusalem was still a thriving, bustling city and the outlying countryside, the Negev and Shephelah, was populated?

Well, that should make things clear for the priests and the people of Jerusalem. As my son would say, "Baaaa Bamm!" Zechariah certainly had a stern answer and convicting response for his people, but let's not skip the lesson that's in here for us.

Our churches and religions still have many traditions we participate in. For example, I never participated in Lent (fasting before Easter) until I asked someone why they participated. "I give up

Hear, O Israel: The LORD our God, the LORD is one. [5] Love the LORD your God with all your heart and with all your soul and with all your strength. [6] These commandments that I give you today are to be on your hearts. [7] Impress them on your children. Talk about them when you sit at home and when you walk along the road, when you lie down and when you get up. [8] Tie them as symbols on your hands and bind them on your foreheads. [9] Write them on the doorframes of your houses and on your gates.

Deuteronomy 6:4-9

something I enjoy each year during Lent as a way to remember the sacrifice Jesus made for me on the cross.", my friend said. Although, giving up TV, Facebook® or sweet tea (in my case) doesn't come close to the sacrifice Jesus made, it acts as a daily reminder of something we might forget or overlook during other times of the year. The unimaginable sacrifice – God sending His only Son to die for us so His blood could cover our sins. It's hard to comprehend how we could lose sight of that so often.

I have also embraced the Jewish tradition of placing a Mezuzah on the door frame of our home. It houses a scroll of parchment paper with Deuteronomy 6:4-9 and 11:13-21 inscribed on it. Each time we enter or exit the house, it is a visual reminder of God's laws, commandments and my responsibility as a Christian and parent. I encourage you to look up this Jewish tradition and read more about it. I have embraced these traditions because they draw my mind and heart back to Christ. I don't participate because it's expected of me or because it will make me a better Christian. I don't participate because everyone else is doing it. I have chosen to adopt these traditions because they draw me closer to my Heavenly Father. They keep my eyes focused on Him.

All of these rituals and traditions are rooted in faith and a desire to draw closer to Christ, but when we allow them to become "fossilized" over time; they become empty actions that slowly erode values. Fossilized means no longer useful, broken down, set in a rigidly conventional pattern of behavior, habits, or beliefs[25]. Our faith and love for the Lord should be purposeful, engaging and joyful . . . far from fossilized.

Pray about the rituals and traditions you have embraced or been taught over the years. If they have become empty traditions with no meaning attached to them, reconsider taking part in them or take time to study the significance behind them so that you can appreciate and grow in Christ as you take part. Brainstorm some of them in the margin.

Some of the traditions I need to evaluate and research are:

DAY SIXTEEN

Welcome back. Let's get back to business. The word of the Lord was still coming to Zechariah. He reminds his people of several precepts their ancestors were taught and makes it clear that these requirements were not just relevant then, but for them as well.[26] In the margin, write out all the requirements the Lord of hosts' reviews with Zechariah in verses 7:8-10.

The Lord was specific. He told them just what He expected and required of them, but they were too stubborn to listen. They "stopped their ears" and "hardened their hearts."

Ah, as people of God we can really "stop our ears" and "harden our heart" to the ways and laws of our Lord. I know I am guilty of this in my life and it wouldn't be possible for my heart to even try to live up to God's ways if He wasn't present and accounted for in my heart.

Look up the following verses and write out how the God's people reacted to His word in these verses.

Jeremiah 7:26

_____

_____

Acts 7:57

_____

_____

Ezekiel 3:9

_____

_____

The Lord

requires us to:

What happens when God's people don't listen? When their hearts become "diamond hard" and they "turn a stubborn shoulder"? (v.14)

_____

Read Nahum 1:3 in the margin. "His way is in

the _____."

The Jewish people brought the Lord's destruction on themselves. The Babylonians only helped Him carry out the whirlwind and scatter them from their "pleasant land" (v.14) which literally means "the land of desire".[27]

I feel like if God, himself, were able to conclude this chapter it would say:

"Yes, continue to mourn and fast during the fifth month because even though the temple is being rebuilt I do not want you to forget why it was destroyed – why your ancestors were scattered and had to leave their land of desire.
They didn't obey my commands! They were stubborn and did not listen. I don't leave the guilty unpunished. Do not forget! Continue to mourn and fast so that your nation and its people never stray from my ways again."

I can't help but think we should carefully consider this warning for ourselves. Our country, founded on God's word, has strayed so far away from Him. It's difficult to imagine He would leave us unpunished. In fact, I have to agree with what Ruth Graham (Billy Graham's wife) said, "If God doesn't punish America, He'll have to apologize to Sodom and Gomorrah." [28] If you aren't familiar with the story of Sodom and Gomorrah I urge you to read it in Genesis 19.

> The Lord is slow to anger, but great in power; the LORD will not leave the guilty unpunished.
> His way is in the whirlwind and the storm, and clouds are the dust of his feet.
>
> Nahum 1:3

DAY SEVENTEEN

Zechariah 8 – Promises & Blessings

Read Zechariah 8:1-8.

How many times is the word jealous used in verse 2?

_____ times

Do you think the Lord was trying to make a point!? I want to stop here for a minute and clarify the meaning behind God's "jealousy". In our society, jealously is looked at as a very negative emotion. We see it as envy and resentment. However, when we see the word jealous used in reference to God's feelings, it means He has extreme, intense, deep and passionate feelings for His people.[29]

Just like a couple renewing their wedding vows, we will see God reminding His people of His great love for them. He will affirm all His promises to bless His chosen nation. Their time of trial and judgment are nearing the end.

Read Ezekiel 37:21 in the margin.

The Lord is going to _____

them (his people) from all around and bring

them to their_____ land.

The Lord is going to gather His people. He is going to scoop them up, draw close to them, harvest them, bring them together and place them in their own land. This is a beautiful image and brings me so much joy to know that our God loves us just as much. So much, that one day He will come to gather us up and take us to live along side of Him, just as He has promised.

"Then say to them, Thus says the Lord God: Behold I will take the people of Israel from the nations among which they have gone, and I will gather them from all around, and bring them to their own land."

Ezekiel 37:21

In verses 1-8, we read about glorious images of God's people having the opportunity to live longer lives and become grandparents. They are able to sit along and enjoy watching the young children play in the streets. They would be a faithful nation again and be blessed by the Lord.

Read Amos 9:14 in the margin and underline the other things God had promised His people.

We are fortunate to see these sites around our towns and neighborhoods and to experience such abundant blessings in the United States. Step back from what you know. Can you imagine how it must have felt for those listening to Zechariah share this message from the Lord of Hosts? These were people who probably felt like residents returning from a hurricane evacuation to find their homes and every inch of their town destroyed. When you are in the middle of such destruction it is difficult to comprehend that it can and will return to what it was before the destruction. How awesome it must have been to hear these promises of hope and assurances of provision from God.

Read Zechariah 8:9-23.

Reread verse 9. Do you remember when the foundation for the temple had been laid?

The work of restoration began around 535 B.C., but was delayed because of the people's discouragement. The rebuilding began around 521 B.C. so it had been about 14 years since the foundation had been laid.[30]

This point of this reminder was to comfort them and bring them assurance. For example, if two people tell you a story and one person was there for the event and the other only heard about it, who are you more likely to believe? Right! The one who was there. The Lord is saying; "Listen to these prophets. They were there when the foundation was laid. You can trust them." And He doesn't stop there. He continues to give them encouragement.

And I will bring my people Israel back from exile. "They will rebuild the ruined cities and live in them. They will plant vineyards and drink their wine; they will make gardens and eat their fruit.

Amos 9:14

We see two phrases that are repeated in these verses. I don't want to skip over them because they are assuring God's people of His blessings to come. "Let your hands be strong" and "fear not". Let your hands be strong means "be of courageous mind."[31]

Look at Haggai 2:5 in the margin. Underline why God's people should "not be afraid". The Spirit of God was in their midst, they need not fear.

Do you ever stop during the day and consider the fact that the Holy Spirit is residing in your heart? Can you sense His tug on your heart as He guides your actions, words and deeds or do you override them?

In the margin, write about a time you felt God nudging you to do or say one thing and how you overrode His nudge and handled it your own way. How did it turn out? How might it have turned out differently if you followed God instead?

After some history and encouragement, the Lord begins giving them a list of things they should do.

Starting in verse 16, list out the actions God wants them to take.

These are the things you shall do:

1. Speak the _____ to one another.

2. Render in your gates judgments that are

   _____ and _____.

3. Do not plot _____ in your hearts against one another.

4. Do not love to _____ falsely.

According to the covenant that I made with you when you came out of Egypt. My Spirit remains in your midst.
Fear not.
Haggai 2:5 (ESV)

God nudged me to

_____
And instead I . . .

For all these things I **HATE** (emphasis mine), declares the Lord. (v.17) Hate is another very strong word, just like jealously. When God uses these words I feel like He is saying it in all caps, in bold and highlighted!

As chapter 8 concludes, we see Zechariah explain that all the fasts they have participated in over the years, to memorialize destruction, will now be fasts of "joy and gladness". We'll take a closer look at those tomorrow.

DAY EIGHTEEN

Let's take a look at each of the fasts and what they represented to God's people. I know this may seem tedious, but when you understand the meaning behind the ceremony it brings the story to life and you begin to see more clearly through the eyes of Zechariah's people. You can always look in the margin if you need a hint.

Fast of the Fourth Month

Read 2 Kings 25:3-4.
What happened during this time?

_____

_____

Fast of the Fifth Month

Read Jeremiah 52:12-15.

What happened to the city of Jerusalem on this day?

_____

Fast of the Seventh Month

Read 2 Kings 25:25.

Who was assassinated? _____

Have you ever used a harsh word to get a strong point across to someone? Did it work?

Fast of the 4th month: when the walls of Jerusalem fell.

Fast of the 5th Month: when the city fell

Fast of the 7th month: when Gedaliah was assassinated

Fast of the 10th month: when the siege of the city began

So, who was this Gedaliah? When Nebuchadnezzar conquered Judah, he didn't want to live there, but he didn't want it to go into complete ruin either. So, he appointed Gedaliah governor over Judah. However, after he was assassinated, it left Judah devoid of any Jews and Jewish rule.[32]

Fast of the Tenth Month

Read 2 Kings 25:1. What began during this time?

_____

These terrible events disrupted and changed their lives for years. Can you imagine what was racing through their minds as they begin to realize that the meaning of all their fasts would now change from remembering despair, to celebrating restoration? Praise God! I imagine Zechariah getting a standing ovation after this declaration sank in.

Can you remember a time when someone did something unexpected that turned your life upside-down? They meant it for harm, but God turned it around and used it for good. Maybe a boss had it out for you at work and you were fired, and God used that opportunity to give you the job of your dreams. Maybe someone broke your heart and you were devastated for months, but God used that opportunity to introduce you to your future spouse. Write down that memory in the margin.

As we close chapter 8, let's take a step back and reflect on everything that the prophet Zechariah has told his people. He shared God's message of history, renewed promises, gave them comfort and told them God would be turning their suffering into joy. Imagine you were in the crowd listening to Zechariah. What feelings do you think you would have experienced as you heard the promises of coming peace and prosperity?

_____

_____

> You intended to harm me, but God intended it for good to accomplish what is now being done, the saving of many lives.
> Genesis 50:20

I remember when:

DAY NINETEEN

How are you feeling as we make approach the half way mark of Zechariah? Take some time to reflect and write out a few themes that have resonated in your heart.

Zechariah 9 – Judgment Day

Can you imagine Zechariah remembering all he saw in these visions to share with his people? I would have asked for a notebook and pen so I could take notes. I am easily distracted. In fact, as I sit and write this I'm distracted by the smell of zucchini bread I'm baking in the oven. Sheesh! No wonder I didn't get the gift of prophesy.

Do you think Zechariah was writing down these things as God revealed them or if they were just so awesome and incredible that the memory was forever burned into his mind? The Lord doesn't reveal Himself to everyone and even the prophets only got glimpses. Now that I think about it, having experienced the Word and presence of God probably doesn't require note taking. It is something you never forget.

We are a little over half way through the book of Zechariah. This study isn't for sissies! Just hearing the word "futuristic prophesy" can be intimidating, so to study a book in the Bible that mirrors Revelation in its imagery, symbols and visions takes courage.

This study has taken me out of my comfort zone but grown my faith and courage in studying scripture. I'm sure there are many other layers to this onion, but we are digging deep and almost done. Don't give up.

These last 6 chapters are full of prophesy, so you will have accomplished much when we reach Zechariah 14:11. I pray one of those things is a bold new desire to study God's word.

Alright, pep talk over. We are going to read chapter 9 in three sections.

Read Zechariah 9:1-8.

You probably noticed the shift as soon as you opened your Bible to chapter 9. Not only is it written differently, it's different for several other reasons. Some commentators believe these last 6 chapters were written well after the first portion of the book. In fact, when these last chapters were written the temple had been completed for years and the Jews had seen God's promises of provision become a reality.[33] We have been reading and studying Zechariah's visions, but chapter 9 is an oracle. An oracle isn't just a revelation or insight about what is to come, but a message or announcement from God.[34]

In verses 1-8 we see that God is announcing His judgment that will fall on Israel's enemies. The Message translation calls it a "war bulletin". Below, list all the places that are going to be devoured and left desolate so Israel no longer has to fear invasions or oppression from them.

My thoughts & feelings on Zechariah 9:8.

1. _____Hadrach_____

2. _____

3. _____

4. _____

5. _____

6. _____

7. _____

8. _____

9. _____Ashdod_____

That's an impressive list. If I lived in any of these cities, I would be shaking. Look at verse 4 and complete it below.

"The Lord will _____ her

_____."

And He doesn't stop there:

"Consumed/devoured by _____"
(v.4)

"Gaza will writhe in _____"
(v. 5)

"Ashkelon will be _____"
(v. 5)

My thoughts . . .

Even in all of this, God is still merciful. Look at verse 7. He will give these people the chance to repent of their ways. What ways, you may ask?

Look up Leviticus 3:17. What does it state that you <u>should</u> <u>not</u> do?

_____

They were blatantly choosing to break God's laws, but He was going to give them a chance to repent and become part of His people.

Look up Isaiah 14:1. What will the sojourners be able to do?

_____

_____

And I love how He closes in verse 8. Read it below from The Message translation.

> **"*I will set up camp in my home country and defend it against invaders. Nobody is going to hurt my people ever again. I'm keeping my eye on them.*"**

As we close today, spend some time reflecting on this last verse. Do you embrace God's defense daily? Do you trust His plan, His presence and His protection? Use the margin to journal your thoughts today.

DAY TWENTY

Your King will come!

Read Zechariah 9:9-17

All I can say after I read this is, "Wow!" Don't forget, we are still in the Old Testament. Jesus hasn't been born or walked this earth, but they are hearing about the promise of a King who will come to save their people.

All of this prophesy is based on what the angel of the Lord is revealing to our prophet Zechariah. Sometimes, I have to remind myself of that. The book we call the Bible is so much more than we realize. It's a collection of stories that are woven together by over forty different authors over a three hundred year period and it all ties together. As a writer, it's hard enough to put a book together by myself; there is no question in my mind that the Bible is God-breathed. No human is capable of master-minding this perfection!

Alright, we'll get started for the day, but I believe it's important to stop and sit in awe God's amazing written Word. Thanks for indulging me.

Who is coming to them according to verse 9?

_____

How will their King arrive? _____

Does that sound familiar at all? Look ahead to the New Testament at Matthew 21:4-5 and John 12:14-15 in the margin. In Matthew, it says this took place to "fulfill what was spoken through the prophet" and in John it says they found Jesus on a donkey "as it is written". Are you getting excited now? As we go through the final five chapters of Zechariah we are going to see several more sneak peeks regarding Jesus' ministry. Don't worry; I'll be sure to point them out. I'm so inspired by these intricate details that tie scripture together.

This took place to fulfill what was spoken through the prophet: "Say to Daughter Zion, See, your king comes to you, gentle and riding on a donkey, and on a colt, the foal of a donkey."
Matthew 21:4-5

Jesus found a donkey and sat on it as is written: "Do not be afraid, Daughter Zion; see, your king is coming, seated on a donkey's colt."
John 12:14-15

The angel continues to share with Zechariah about what this coming King will do. Look at verse 10.

What will He speak/proclaim to the nations?

_____

He will rule from _____ to _____

and to the ends of the _____.

There is another verse I want us to pay close attention to. In verse 11, he calls them "prisoners of hope".

The definition of prisoner is "a person held in custody, captivity, or a condition of forcible restraint."[35] I can't think of anything I would rather be held captive to more than hope. As Christians, our hope in the Lord our God comes from the confidence we have in knowing, believing, and trusting in Him.

These hope-filled prisoners were getting some amazing news. Step out of yourself for a moment and sit in the crowd with them as they listen. Imagine all of the trials, anguish, pain and disruption their families had endured. Now imagine them standing as they listen to Zechariah share the message from God. A spectacular message that included the promise of a coming King that would save them and restore their nation. Not only will He appear and bring restoration, but His arrow will flash like lightening, His trumpet will sound, He will shield them, save them, and overcome their enemies with only a slingshot because that is our God! (v.14-17) He is awesome! He is able! He is mighty! He is just! He is truth! He is light! He is faithful! He is merciful! He is our KING! Can I get an "Amen!"

As we close out chapter 9 today, the question I have for you is this ~ Are you a prisoner of hope or a prisoner of doubt? Take a look in the margin and ponder what hope is and what it is not before you decide.

Hope is:

anticipation

assumption belief

confidence

dependence

desire

endurance

expectancy

faith

optimism

promise

reliance

security

Hope is not:

despair

disbelief

discouragement

hopelessness

pessimism

uncertain

skeptical

So many times, we think we are prisoners of hope and then when a crisis hits we realize we had deceived ourselves or the enemy had lulled us into complacency that brought on more disbelief and hopelessness than hope.

If you are feeling more like a prisoner of hopelessness today. There is a solution. Ask God for help. Pray for him to restore your passion, adoration, hope and desire for Him. He listens, He loves, He answers and He would love nothing more than to give you the desires of your heart.

DAY TWENTY-ONE

Rebuilding

Read Zechariah 10:1-12.

The world tells us that in order to love, we have to support what others think and do. With "worldly love" you can't have a differing opinion. It says that "you must agree to love". The world says love means following and doing what everyone else does, but the LOVE that God teaches and shows is completely different.

Look at Zechariah 10:6 in the margin and write out the things God is promising the people of Judah. I've given you the first letter of each word. I will:

S_____ Judah

R_____ them

A_____ them

God's love provides strength, restoration and saves. Why? Verse 6 tells us. Because the Lord has compassion, He will answer them.

Read Isaiah 14:1 in the margin. What will the Lord have for his people?

"I will strengthen Judah and save the tribes of Joseph. I will restore them because I have compassion on them. They will be as though I had not rejected them, for I am the LORD their God and I will answer them.
Zechariah 10:6

The LORD will have compassion on Jacob; once again he will choose Israel and will settle them in their own land. Foreigners will join them and unite with the descendants of Jacob.
Isaiah 14:1 (NIV)

Compassion is defined as a "deep awareness of the suffering of another coupled with the wish to relieve it."[36]

You know those days or maybe even weeks when you find yourself worn out from it all? The good news seems like a train that left the station weeks ago and is yet to return. That is what these people had been feeling for years and years! But God heard their call and Zechariah urged his people to get rid of all the idols that had been a large part of their past and present. He wanted them to trust in God completely again, even for the rain. (v.1) Why? Because God was aware of their suffering and was ready to relieve it. Now was the time!

Do you think they believed Zechariah right away? They had been waiting on God to deliver them for so long. Do you think they had forgotten God stands in center of it all? Have you forgotten?

Have you forgotten that His glory and beautiful promises of rest, peace, mercy and protection shine their brightest during the dark and cold moments of life? We want to hurry past the hard stuff. Get through it. Move on. We don't like the pruning. The wait. It's hard. It hurts. It doesn't make sense. But, it's in the wait that God does His best work in us. Where we grow the most. It's in the harshest of life's challenges He endures and uses His power to produce fruit when all odds seem against it. Nothing is impossible for Him. Nothing! He offers hope. The hope that greater things are to come. Hope that happiness will triumph over sadness and despair. Hope that forgiveness will enter and reign in a bitter heart. Hope that peace will prevail over our weary and stressful lives. Hope that love will conquer all.

Have you been waiting on something from the Lord? Restoration from a dysfunctional relationship, a drug addiction, loneliness, depression, illness, or just more passion in your life for Him?

Use the margin to write out what you are waiting on from God.

Now, let's go back to the question I asked before. Do you think they believed Zechariah right away? If I was sitting down with you right now and offered you words of encouragement that God was coming, He had heard your cry and was going to show compassion. Would you believe me?

I'm sure Zechariah struggled with this as a leader and prophet. How could he make them believe? How many visions would he have to share before it sank it? Was he making a difference? Was anyone listening? The important thing was that Zechariah knew for sure that God would come through and thankfully he didn't give up or give in. He kept sharing his visions and prophecy of hope and promise of the coming King.

Dear Lord, I'm really waiting on:

DAY TWENTY-TWO

Let's look closer at Zechariah 10:8 today.

What three things is the Lord going to do for His people?

_____ them

_____ them

_____ them

So, not only is He going to provide them strength, restoration and save them (as we learned yesterday), but He is also going to signal, gather and redeem them. This just keeps getting better! Let's take a closer look at these words.

Signal ~ The Lord is going to signal them. This literally means "to whistle".[37] Look up Isaiah 5:26. What does God do for those at the ends of the earth? He whistles for them! How precious and awesome. Just like shepherds call to their sheep and we call our children, pets and friends, so the Lord will call to us. Even those at the ends of the earth will not be forgotten, but signaled and called home.

Gather ~ The Lord is going to gather them. Even though He scattered them (v. 9) and despite seas of trouble (v.11) the Lord is promising to care for Judah and assemble His people once again. And finally, He promises to . . .

Redeem ~ The Lord is promising to pay the price for their sins so love, forgiveness and eternal life will be theirs.

We don't have to believe Zechariah. We know the end of the story. We know our God comes through. He sends His son, Jesus to die on the cross as payment for our sins. I think at this point, if I had been listening to Zechariah I would have been getting goose bumps.
I would have felt the faith returning and the trust growing. Signal, gather and redeem! Are you believing?

DAY TWENTY-THREE

Dooms Day

Read Zechariah 11:1-17.

I know! I didn't get it at first either, but stick with me. There are a few key details that will help us unwrap this chapter and actually understand it.

First Key
Unlike chapter 10, we see Zechariah shift his attention from the flock (people of Israel) to those who are shepherding the flock.

"I am the good shepherd. The good shepherd lays down his life for the sheep.
John 10:11

"I am the good shepherd; I know my sheep and my sheep know me—
John 10:14

"Very truly I tell you Pharisees, anyone who does not enter the sheep pen by the gate, but climbs in by some other way, is a thief and a robber.
John 10:1

In the ESV translation, this chapter is titled "The Flock Doomed to Slaughter".

That will get your attention! I imagine all the faces in the crowd and see the look of confusion and shock as Zechariah changes gears from promises, care, and love to slaughter. They are beginning to see that Zechariah is not just the prophet of hope; he is also the prophet of truth.[38] As we move through these verses you will begin to understand why the Lord's attitude is so harsh.

Second Key
This is another sign act (or action item) just like we saw in Zechariah 6. Look closely at Zechariah 11:4. It's easy to miss if you don't study other Bible translations.

In the ESV translation this verse reads, "Thus said the Lord my God: Become shepherd of the flock doomed to slaughter". The Lord is actually instructing Zechariah to act out these verses and pretend he is the shepherd to this flock that is described as "doomed to slaughter".[39] Bring out the drama team, right? Maybe the Lord knew this was going to be <u>way</u> to confusing unless they saw it acted out as a play. I get that. So far, this chapter has required more study and prayer than any other chapter in Zechariah for me.

Third Key
Who are the two shepherds referenced in chapter 11? By looking at verses 4 and 7 we see that Zechariah is told to play one of the shepherds. This is the Good Shepherd who will give His life for His sheep.[40] But then, another shepherd is introduced in verse 16. He is presented as the foolish shepherd, who represents the antichrist.[41]

I know! I know! It's getting deep in here. Maybe after this study, Revelation will seem like a piece of cake. We'll stop for today and pick up where we left off tomorrow. Don't give up . . . it's getting good.

Use the margin to recap or draw some illustrations to help process all we learned today.

Notes:

DAY TWENTY-FOUR

Read Zechariah 11:4-17 again. Maybe now that your brain has had some time to absorb the background for these verses they make a little more sense when you read them. Let's start in verse 7 and take a closer look at the Good Shepherd. He became their shepherd and tended them with two staffs.

Write out the names of the two staffs below.

_____ & _____

I did some research into the staff names. I looked at several different Bible translations to compare words and terminology. Check out the margin. It gives us a clearer picture of what favor and union really meant to Zechariah and his people. You could also look at them as the staffs of grace and covenants.[42] Not only does the good shepherd take over with favor and grace, in just one month he destroys three other shepherds (v. 8). Who are these other shepherds? Well, there are a lot of different thoughts on this, but the overall theme is that the other shepherds were false prophets. Not bad for just a month in office!

Then, just one verse later the shepherd quits. In verse 8 he says the flock _____ me.

The shepherd breaks the staff of _____ in verse 10. This symbolizes a break in covenant he had made with them and all the nations.

Stop the press! What does this mean? Did this hit you, like it did me? God (who this shepherd is representing) tells us over and over that He won't break his covenant with us. So what's the deal here? I think Vernon McGee explains it best.

> "Well, we need to understand the
> difference between a conditional and

Favor
Beauty (KJV)
Delight (CE)
Lovely (Message)

Union
Bands (KJV)
Harmony (CE & Message)

an unconditional covenant. God never breaks an unconditional covenant. But a conditional covenant depends upon a response from the human side. The covenant of the verse before us is conditional. God's promised protections of Israel against their enemies depended upon Israel's obedience to Him. When they disobeyed Him, he followed through by removing protection. It is in this sense that He broke His covenant."[43]

Here is where it gets really good. Read verse 13 again. How many pieces of silver was the shepherd given for his wages? _____

What did he do with it?

_____

Does this sound familiar to you? Read Matthew 27:1-10 in the margin.

How many pieces of silver did Judas receive to betray Jesus? _____

What did Judas do with them before he hung himself?

_____

And people say the Bible is boring. This is an incredible prophesy that is fulfilled in such a unique way. Like I said before, no other author could pull this off.

Thirty pieces of silver was equivalent to less than minimum wage. About what a slave made back then. Can you imagine how humiliating and disappointing this must have been? He had come with staffs of favor and union, destroyed false prophets and then became despised.

This reminds me of a terrible work place situation. You are hired, come in with great gusto, fresh ideas and give it your all, but people start to hate and resent you for it. You finally rip up the contract, quit, and leave them to their own devices. You get a lousy severance, waste it on a

When Judas, who had betrayed him, saw that Jesus was condemned, he was seized with remorse and returned the thirty pieces of silver to the chief priests and the elders. [4] "I have sinned," he said, "for I have betrayed innocent blood."

Matthew 27:3-4

shopping spree and then break the second staff. OK, you probably wouldn't break the second staff, but that's what the good shepherd did.

He broke the second staff, which was the staff of union. This symbolized the covenant between the Shepherd and Israel (his flock) being broken. It's like God was saying, "You sold me out, you turned your back on me, rejected me and had me crucified, so our covenant is broken and you will be scattered around the world."[44] And you know what? They still are.

In verse 16, what does the shepherd say he is rising up?

_____

_____

So, here enters our "symbolic" antichrist into the play. Verse 16 describes him as one who does not care, does not heal, does not nourish, but one who devours and tears. Not the kind of shepherd you would advertise for if given the option, right?

Thankfully, the glorious image we get to close on today is verse 17, where we read that the Lord (our Good Shepherd) will finish off this worthless shepherd.

Fill in the words from verse 17.

The sword will strike his _____ and

his right _____.

The arm and his eye are symbolic because they are parts of the body that are critical to doing his nasty job in warfare and controlling his flock.[45] So these injuries are vital to his demise. Our God is always thinking ahead.

As we close today, reflect on the verses in the margin from the book of John.

Jesus answered, "I told you, but you don't believe. Everything I have done has been authorized by my Father, actions that speak louder than words. You don't believe because you're not my sheep. My sheep recognize my voice. I know them, and they follow me. I give them real and eternal life. They are protected from the Destroyer for good. No one can steal them from out of my hand. The Father who put them under my care is so much greater than the Destroyer and Thief. No one could ever get them away from him. I and the Father are one heart and mind." John 10:25-30 (The Message)

DAY TWENTY-FIVE

Before you read today, let's get a little background. A new section of Zechariah's prophecy begins in Chapter 12. In fact, chapters 12-14 are things that we have not yet seen fulfilled. We have seen everything up until this point fulfilled in the scripture. But, the prophesies we are getting ready to study in the remaining chapters refer to the second coming of Christ. The time of Great Tribulation. That's right. Hidden here, in this Old Testament book, is some good ol' "end times" prophesy. Good thing you didn't know that when we started this study, right?

A little disclaimer here! Scholars and commentary gurus disagree on a lot on end times details. There are several different schools of thought so please dig deeper on your own if this interest you. If you do, you will find there are those who think God will return for believers before the Great Tribulation, others who think we will be here to endure it and others who are somewhere in between. I'll spare you all the fancy names and details, but it is fascinating if you want to dig deeper.

Now that you have a little more context, please read Zechariah 12:1-9.

Did you notice it? Here is our second oracle. Remember, we saw our first oracle in Zechariah 9. This message from God in chapter 12 is a description of the Great Tribulation.[46] What in the world is the Great Tribulation you ask?

The English word *tribulation* means great distress, misery, affliction and/or persecution. According to many prophecy teachers, this isn't just referring to an indeterminate time period, but rather to a specific time period they call the Tribulation. The most common speculation, based on comparing prophetic passages in the Bible, is that it will last for seven years. Some of these teachers refer to the whole seven years as The Great Tribulation. Others prefer not to consider the first half of the seven years as being "great" but only the second half, when circumstances on Earth become even more horrifying and miserable."[47]

I know this may seem a little intimidating, but if you'll stick with me, we will begin to see some amazing things in these verses that seem pretty foreign at first glance. Let's break down verse 1. There are three incredible things within this one verse. Three awesome statements concerning our Creator.

Fill in the blanks. "The Lord, who . . .

1._____

2._____

3._____

Our God, our Creator stretched out the heavens, laid the foundation of the earth and formed the spirit of all men/women. The Message translation reads this way.

"GOD's Message concerning Israel, GOD's Decree—the very GOD who threw the skies into space, set earth on a firm foundation, and breathed his own life into men and women:"

What an awesome reminder of who our God is, was, and always will be. I don't think it's a mistake that He starts out His message this way. When you are about to make an announcement that you know will seem like a stretch to those listening – what better way to start out than by reminding them of who our God is. He is the Master and Creator of all people and things. So, surely this is all in His capable hands.

You know when you are about to tell a friend about something miraculous or strange that happened to you? You might start with a statement like, "I know this will sound crazy, but . . . ." I feel like that's what God is doing here. Maybe He said, "I know this will sound far-fetched Zechariah, but I am the God of all

"For then there will be great tribulation, such as has not been since the beginning of the world until this time, no, nor ever shall be."
Matthew 24:21, (NKJV)

creation, so just keep that in mind as you listen. Nothing is out of my control" And once He has reminded them of that, in verse 2 (in several translations) it says "Behold". In other words, "Watch out for this!"

Are you getting goose bumps yet? God's word is so brilliant.

So, what are we watching out for? We'll break it down tomorrow.

DAY TWENTY-SIX

As promised yesterday, let's break it down. What are we to "behold" or watch out for?

In verse 2, Jerusalem is going to be made into a cup that sends people _____.

In the ESV translation, it says they will be a "cup of staggering" and in the King James it says "a cup of trembling". Some commentators even think this means Jerusalem will become the very place where the Antichrist takes over.[48]

In verse 3, all the nations will gather against Jerusalem, but the Lord will make her an immovable _____.

Read Matthew 7:24-25 in the margin. What happens when the Lord is our rock?

_____

_____

In Zechariah 12:5 it says, "the people of Jerusalem are strong because

_____

_____

Therefore everyone who hears these words of mine and puts them into practice is like a wise man who built his house on the rock. 25 The rain came down, the streams rose, and the winds blew and beat against that house; yet it did not fall, because it had its foundation on the rock.
Matthew 7:24-25 (NIV)

Have you gotten tired of reading "In that day" yet? It's mentioned 7 times in chapter 12 alone. It's also translated as "on the big day" in the Message. It will be a big day! Fill in the following words that are missing from the remaining verses.

Verse 7 "The LORD will save the

_____ of Judah first, so that the honor of the house of David and of Jerusalem's inhabitants may not be greater than that of Judah.

Verse 8 "In that day the LORD will _____ those who live in Jerusalem, so that the feeblest among them will be like David, and the house of David will be like God, like the angel of the LORD going before them."

Verse 9, "On that day I will set out to

_____ all the nations that

_____ Jerusalem.

Verse 10, "And I will pour out on the house of David and the inhabitants of Jerusalem a spirit

of _____ and

_____.

In the margin, write out all the words you just used to fill in the scriptures for verses 8–10.

The Lord is going to shield, honor, protect from Them from all enemies and pour grace and mercy onto them and then, they will get it!

Look at the final verses (v. 10-14) from the Message translation.

"They'll then be able to recognize me as the One they so grievously wounded—that piercing spear-thrust! And they'll weep— oh, how they'll weep! Deep mourning as of

Words from Zechariah 12:7-10 activity:

1.

2.

3.

4.

5.

a parent grieving the loss of the firstborn child. The lamentation in Jerusalem that day will be massive, as famous as the lamentation over Hadad-Rimmon (see margin) **on the fields of Megiddo: Everyone will weep and grieve, the land and everyone in it: The family of David off by itself and their women off by themselves;** . . .

Everyone's family will go off by themselves and grieve for what they should have seen so many generations before. Jesus was and is their Messiah. The one and only Son of God.

Thanks for hanging in there. I know this has been a long day of study. As we close, reflect on this:

Have you ever grieved and wept over your sins? Have you ever gotten down on your knees before God and felt overwhelmed by the disappointment and frustration over that sin? We are new in Christ every day, but let's not forget how much it hurts Him when we sin. Let's grieve for our sins, truly repent and turn them over to God because that's when we receive complete healing and restoration through Him. Let's take care of it now, so we aren't lamenting on the day of His return but instead celebrating His glorious return.

What was Hadad-Rimmon and why were they so sad there?

It's the name of the town near Megiddo where an intense battle occurred and King Josiah died while fighting. You can read more about it in 2 Chronicles 35:20-24.

DAY TWENTY-SEVEN

We have covered a lot of information so let's recap for a moment. Zechariah has shared a lot of prophesy with us so far. The end result will be eternal peace, joy and happiness with our Lord, but we have to work our way to that. Like most things, it won't come without a little work.

When Jesus came, He was rejected and died a criminal's death. Since that time, we have been able to enjoy the benefits of having the Holy Spirit dwell within us.

Zechariah has shown us that a time will come when the "worthless shepherd" (a.k.a. Antichrist) will come along and make big promises, but bring nothing more than the Great Tribulation. All part of God's master plan that will lead to the destruction of the Antichrist and the establishment of God's perfect kingdom here on earth.

In day 26, we found that God's chosen people would realize their wrong and go off alone to lament and grieve their sin of disbelief. We hate to be wrong, don't we? And this is a BIG one. I imagine all the looks on their faces when it finally registers that Jesus really was (and is) the Son of God. Can you see the looks of terror, shock and sadness? What are some other emotions that come to mind as you imagine this scene? It would be like discovering you had the winning lottery ticket for years and found it the day after it expired.

In chapter 13, we will see how God is going to cleanse them from their sins. How He is going to get in those hearts, help them face the sin and clean it up for them?

Read Zechariah 13:1-6.

There it is again, right there is verse 1, "On that day". On the big day, what will be opened to the house of David and Jerusalem's inhabitants?

_____

Read Ezekiel 36:25 in the margin. What will sprinkling them with water do?

_____

_____

The Lord is getting ready to do some cleaning! Look at verse 2. What will be banished or removed?

_____

I will sprinkle clean water on you, and you will be clean; I will cleanse you from all your impurities and from all your idols.

Ezekiel 36:25

Once and for all, the Lord is going to rid this place of all its idols and false prophets. False prophets are those who say their actions are of God's power, but are actually controlled by demons. This verse is important because it is the only place in the Bible that talks about God kicking demons out of here "on that day". Revelation tells us Satan and the Antichrist will be put down in a lake of fire and the bottomless pit, but never mentions demons will join them.[49] I just assumed the demons would go along with Satan and the Antichrist, but it's nice to know for sure.

Verse 3 is hard core. What are the parents supposed to do if their son or daughter continues to share prophesies?

_____

Whoa! Stab them. Pierce them. Thrust them. Stab them to death. Doesn't really matter what translation you read, they all mean the same. That's tough stuff. I don't care if your teenager did just yell at you before she left for school this morning and screamed, "I hate you."

Look up Luke 14:26. What feeling must we have towards ourselves and our families if we want to be a disciple of Christ?

_____

I know what you are thinking. What happened to the love? I thought we were called to love everyone and show Christ's love through our love. We are. Sorry, we aren't getting out of that one.

God is explaining that in this new time (on that day) hearts will be transformed and our first priority will be the Lord. This is relevant in our lives today because when we make our spouses or children idols and place them before God we are only setting them up for attack from the enemy. Trust God with them today! They are not ours. They are only on loan from Him just like everything else we have in our possession.

Some idols I need to turn over are:

Finances
Materialism
Shopping
Appearance
Children
Husband
Singleness
Inability to have children
Computer time
Work
Social status

What else do you think about more than God? Write them out and put them under the fountain today.

Verse 6 got my attention so I did some digging. Notice the question. "What are these wounds on your body?" In the ESV and KJ translations it reads, "What are these wounds on your back?" But, in Hebrew the word is "yâd" which means hand.[50] Some commentators actually think the "him" they are speaking to, is Christ himself.[51] Like I said, some commentators. Others believe they are referring to the false prophets who have scars from pagan rituals.[52] Apparently, it's not just this verse, but the remaining three chapters of Zechariah that are controversial. When there is controversy, you are usually onto something.

Look at the end of verse 6, where did the wounds come from?

In the "house of friends". Does that strike a cord with you?

A friend is defined as a person whom one knows, likes, and trusts. A person with whom one is allied in a struggle or cause; a comrade and one who supports, sympathizes with you.[53]

Christ certainly died by the hands of those who waved Him into Jerusalem with palm branches and cheers and then turned on Him. It breaks my heart and fills it with joy at the same time. What a mighty God we serve.

The wild part of all this is, there were those who didn't believe then, there are those who don't believe now and even "on that day" there will still be those who don't believe.

Do you believe today? I mean, really believe? Have Satan's lies overcome God's whispers? Take a few minutes today and ask God reveal any doubt, fear, sin or other emotion that is getting in the way of you believing in Him today! Let's not wait for "that day" when there is so much He wants to give you now.

We'll finish the rest of chapter 13 tomorrow. Your time with God can't wait!

A side note:

I can see how commentators have differing opinions about who the "him" with wounds in verse 6 is referring to. In verse 5 they are talking about false prophets and in verse 7 they are talking about Christ with verse 6 sandwiched in between. There are just some things we won't know until God's Kingdom reigns on Earth and we finally get to sit down and have a chat with Him. I wonder if I'll even be able to form a sentence?

DAY TWENTY-EIGHT

In many Bibles, this segment of chapter 13 is titled the shepherd struck and the sheep scattered. So, hold onto your seats as we dive into these final verses. We are only looking at three verses today so it will be short and sweet.

Read Zechariah 13:7-9.

We see here that the Lord is speaking about Christ, our Savior and His son. He calls Him:

The man that is my fellow (KJV)
The man who stands next to me (ESV)
The man who is close to me (NIV)
My associate (NASB)

This time the sword strikes the "good shepherd" for the promise of our future. After His death, His sheep will be scattered and they are still awaiting His return to be gathered up.

Look up Matthew 26:31 and write it in the margin. What is Jesus saying here? Do you notice a repeated phrase? Underline it. His death brings on a domino effect. Let's take a look.

Domino One falls:

The Shepherd is struck by the sword.

The sheep are _____. (v.7)

Two thirds will be cut off and

_____ (v. 8).

One third will get to live, but that third will be

put into the _____(v.9)

to be _____ and

_____.

The dominos continue to fall, but after they are refined and tested, I sense stillness. All becomes quiet. Then, they will get it. They will wake up and they will call His name and He will answer (v.9). He will say, "They are my people" and they will say,

"The LORD is my God."

What do you need from the Lord today? What answer have you been waiting for? You are one of His chosen people. A part of His holy family. The Lord is *YOUR* God! Spend some time soaking that in before you move on to your "to do" list today. Seek Him for the peace, the healing, the answers, the direction, the advice, the comfort and the love he is waiting to give.

DAY TWENTY-NINE

Well, here we are. Only one chapter and two days left. This journey is almost complete.

Read Zechariah 14:1-11.

I think if we look at these eleven verses in three sections: Judgment, deliverance and exaltation[54] it will help us break them down and see the joy through the pain. Prophesy is the one place you get to see the big picture.

First comes judgment.
Look at verses 1-2. There is plenty in these three verses to make your head turn. You certainly don't want to be on the wrong side of God! Amen!

The final curtain call, that last battle for Jerusalem. All the nations will gather against them for the final battle. List the three main things that will occur during the battle.

1. The city will be taken

2. _____

3. _____

The

Lord

is

YOUR

God!

Soak it in!

Ah, but then there will be deliverance. . .
What is the Lord going to do in verse 3?

_____

Yes, the mighty deliverer. He will come and fight against all the nations on behalf of Jerusalem.

Who will stand on the Mount of Olives and split it in two according to verse 4? _____

That's right, don't miss it. Zechariah is saying that the Lord will be standing on the Mount of Olives and split it right in two with a mighty earthquake. It's through the valley He creates with the earthquake, that His people will escape the devastating invasion they are facing.

Ever had to climb a hill at the end of a run or bike ride? The last few hills are always the most difficult because you are tired, hot, worn out and thirsty. That's when you need a little earthquake to part the hill so you can just take the middle, flat road.

I imagine God seeing His people tired and in desperate need of escape from their final battle, so He creates the perfect valley for them to travel through. No more mountains for them. And finally, exaltation!

"Then the Lord my God will come, and all the holy ones (army of angels) with Him." (v.5)

This is where I feel like standing up in my chair and cheering, "Yeah, God!!! Bring it!" And oh, it gets better. Verse 6 says it going to be "unique" day where there is neither

_____ or _____.

I'm no expert and some may think this book of the Bible may be a little above my pay grade, but it seems to me that this is a definite reference about God's return. Look up Revelation 21:23. What does it say about the need for the sun and moon?

_____

_____

To read more about the earthquake from the days of Uzziah king of Judah mentioned in Zechariah 14:5 check out Amos 1:1-2 below.

The words of he words of Amos, one of the shepherds of Tekoa—the vision he saw concerning Israel two years before the earthquake, when Uzziah was king of Judah and Jeroboam son of Jehoash was king of Israel.
He said, "The LORD roars from Zion and thunders from Jerusalem;
the pastures of the shepherds dry up,
and the top of Carmel withers."

How about Revelation 21:25?

_____

That's right. I feel another "Ba-Bamm" coming. Our God needs no artificial light because HE is the LIGHT! The light of the world!

Not only that, but what will flow out from Jerusalem to the western and eastern seas continuously? (v. 8)

_____

Look up Revelation 22:1. What did the angel show them? _____

But wait, it keeps getting better!

And, the Lord will be King over the _____ earth. (v. 9)

Not just half or part or some, but ALL of it. The whole land will remain plain, but

_____

will remain raised up. (v.10)

Read Isaiah 2:2 in the margin. How does this go along with what Zechariah said?

_____

_____

We are almost done for today. Just one more nugget to exalt over! Look at verse 11 and fill in the blanks below.

Jerusalem will never be _____

again and will forever be _____.

I know that all of this is prophesy. Prophesy about what will happen when Christ returns to claim what is already His, but I think this is a glorious image of what He did for us on the cross too.

In the last days, the mountain of the LORD's temple will be established as the highest of the mountains; it will be exalted above the hills, and all nations will stream to it.

Isaiah 2:2

He was destroyed for our destructive sins so that we can dwell in the security of His love, mercy, grace and forgiveness all the days of our lives.

Now, do you feel like throwing out a "Ba-Bamm!"?

Use the margin, to reflect on your thoughts from today.

DAY THIRTY

I can't believe this is our last day. It's been quite a journey for me. I pray this has grown your courage in studying scripture and your faith in the Lord. Let's finish it up and watch as God humbles the nations a little more after their grim defeat!

Read Zechariah 14:12-21.

The first thing I notice is that there is a lot of rotting flesh in chapter 12. I think it's fair to say it's not looking good around those other nations. So, I understand verse 13 when it tells us that "a great panic from the Lord shall fall on them." I think if they didn't get it after He split the Mount of Olives, they are probably getting it now.

All the wealth from surrounding nations will be brought to Jerusalem and then a plague will fall.

What three items will be brought to Jerusalem? (v.14)

1._____

2._____

3._____

What will fall victim to the plague? (v.15)

_____

_____

Since tomorrow is our last day, take some time to reflect back on all you have studied. What part(s) made you want to yell out a "Ba-Bamm!"?

But, all the survivors get to go up year after year to worship the King, the Lord of Hosts. Can you imagine the privilege of this? They will keep the Feast of Booths, (v. 16) which is the Feast of Tabernacles (see the margin for more on the feast of Tabernacles from Leviticus) which the Israelites celebrated when they came out of Egypt.[55]

If the nations choose not to go up before the Lord and celebrate the Feast of Booths what two things will occur? (v. 17-19)

_____ and _____

Read verses 20-21 one more time as we finish today and let it sink in.

When God reigns on this earth again, everything from the horse bells to the dishes will be holy and used for worship and His glory. Every "trader", unbeliever, hypocrite, critic and wolf in sheep's clothing will be removed! I can only imagine!

Holy to the LORD!

CONCLUSION

Thirty days! We did it! We started as ordinary, but I think this journey has made us all extraordinary! I can't believe we are done. I don't know about you, but God has stretched my knowledge, my desire and my ability to seek Him more and more with each day of this study. I trusted God completely when He placed the book of Zechariah on my heart. Not really knowing much about it until diving in with you. I'm so glad I didn't know how challenging it would be to study and decipher visions and end time prophesies or this study would have ever been written.

"So, summing up: On the fifteenth day of the seventh month, after you have brought your crops in from your fields, celebrate the Feast of GOD for seven days. The first day is a complete rest and the eighth day is a complete rest. On the first day, pick the best fruit from the best trees; take fronds of palm trees and branches of leafy trees and from willows by the brook and celebrate in the presence of your GOD for seven days—yes, for seven full days celebrate it as a festival to GOD.
Leviticus 23:39-41 (MSG)

I say this to encourage you, because so often we want God to lay out the whole plan for us. We want Him to make it easy. We want to know every step before we take just one.
I'm learning that we don't get the whole plan because if we did we would probably run for the hills. Remember, we can't, but God can! Expect anything!

Like Mark Batterson says, "The issue isn't whether you are qualified, but are you called?" Don't miss out on what God is calling you to do because of fear. Don't wait to act "on that day" ~ act TODAY!

Go for it!

Is there something God has been calling you to do that you have been running away from?

Write the worst things that could happen if you follow His lead and then turn all the fear over to Him.

Zechariah ~
10-week group Bible study

Zechariah is a great individual Bible study, but can also be done together in a group format over 10 weeks. You don't have to follow the following break down exactly. It's just a guide. I have included some discussion questions to get you started each week, but please <u>only</u> use them to get started. My hope is that you will star, highlight and underline what touches you through the study and that will be the main discussion for your group.

The first few weeks will have more homework because it's easier to study all the visions from the first section of Zechariah as closely together as you can. After that, the days spread out and there isn't as much homework from week to week.

I would love to hear how the book of Zechariah impacts your group and you personally. You can contact me through my website at **www.allisonTcain.com**.

I pray it grows your trust in God, renews your desire to seek Him in every detail of your life and share His word and love with those you come in contact with.

Blessings,
Allison

Week 1 – Days 1-3

1. Spend time thinking about the people Zechariah is there to encourage, Read 2 Kings 25:1-25 together and discuss how it must have felt to be taken prisoner and forced to leave your home and country. How about your feelings of leaving Babylon to return after being held captive in a city that had now become your home after 70 years?

2. Discuss some of the idols that have a hold on you and make a commitment to prayer for one another to overcome them.

3. How did it make you feel to realize the Lord has His Heavenly troops patrolling the earth?

Week 2 – Days 4-8

1. What do you need a craftsman from God in your life for right now?

2. Had you ever considered or imagined the Lord having a wall of fire around you? How would it change your faith, your daily life and your desire to serve the Lord?

3. Share a time when the Lord probably had to defend your actions to Satan, but loved you and redeemed you by using what Satan meant to harm you for His glory.

Week 3– Days 9-14

1. Which one of the visions studied today meant the most to you and why?

2. What scripture is highlighted, starred and circled in your homework because it's just what you needed to hear. Share it with your group and discuss.

3. How do you stop the temptation of anger, gossip, etc. when faced with a sinful situation?

Week 4 – Days 15 – 18

1. What traditions do you need to evaluate and revisit? Are there any you need to add?
2. Have you ever experienced a time in your life when you "stopped your ears" and "hardened your heart" to the Lord? What was going on in your life? How did He draw you back to Him?
3. What did you share at the end of day 18 when asked to imagine being in the crowd listening to all Zechariah had to share from the angel of the Lord?

Week 5 – Days 19 – 20

1. Read Zechariah 9:9-17 together as a group and discuss the emotions you felt after reading it.
2. Discuss what you think of prisoner of hope looks like, acts like and pray like.
3. Share whether you are a prisoner of hope or doubt, share why and ask your group members to pray for those who are prisoners of doubt to overcome that stronghold and be filled with hope.

Week 6 – Days 21 – 22

1. Read Isaiah 30:18 from the margin of day 21 together. Is anyone waiting on God for something?
   Share and pray for one another.
2. What did you learn about God from reading the verses from the book of John in day 22?
3. Discuss gather and redeem. How did it make you feel to realize your Heavenly Father wants to gather you up – no matter where you are or where you have been and redeem you?

Week 7 – Days 23 – 24

1. Zechariah 11 can start out confusing. Did the keys help you unlock the meaning? What did you learn?
2. Was it fun to find the connection between Zechariah and Matthew 27? Share your thoughts about that and the other places you have seen scripture tie together.
3. Read John 10:25-30 from the margin of day 24 and discuss what means the most to you from that verse.

Week 8 – Days 25 – 26

1. Share a way that God has shielded, honored, and protected you from sin or the enemy himself.
2. Discuss grieving your sins. Have you grieved your sins? How? Did it change you?
3. Take some time as a group or privately (depending on how close your group is) to share or write out your sins and grieve them, confess them and turn them over to God. This is a great time, if you are able, to take communion together.

Week 9 – Days 27-28

1. Have you ever been betrayed by someone you trusted? Do you carry those emotions of distrust over into your relationship with God? If so, how has it held you back in your walk with Christ?
2. What are you ready for the Lord to clean out of your heart and mind? Why are you ready now?

3. Get together with a prayer partner in the group and release those thing to the Lord. He will replace your filthy garments with clean ones.

Week 10 – Days 29-30

1. What verse stood out to you the most this week? Why?
2. What have you felt God calling you to do, but have dismissed out of fear?
3. Reflecting back on the book of Zechariah, what message will you take away? What vision resonated with you the most?

I pray you are completing this study encouraged and feeling more loved by God than you ever had. He is walking with you and will not forsake you. Fall into His arms with full abandon.

ACKNOWLEDEMENTS

I always have to start by thanking my Heavenly Father. He never ceases to amaze me, inspire me and challenge me. Your Word is so relevant, so alive and so real. From my knees, I thank you!

To Eleanor and Kelly, who despite sickness, family emergencies, and life took the time to read and provide me feedback on this Bible study. I adore you both and so blessed and encouraged by you.

To Julie, thank you for helping me create and teach this Bible study. It's always nice to find someone you can trust so completely and work so well with. I'll be your wing man anytime!

To the VineLife girls, Thank you for spending 10 weeks in the book of Zechariah with Julie and me. It was thrilling to see your revelations, hear your questions and share life with you. You helped shape this study into what it is.

To Jenn and Kent, no book is complete without a great editor and the perfect cover. I'm so thankful God led me to the two of you. Thanks for making Zechariah what it is.

And to my awesome mom & dad, husband, children, Leadership girls, small group, LeadHers, neighbors, mentors, friends and blog followers . . . your prayers, support and encouragement are what keep me going on some days.

May we all continue to find encouragement, strength and faith to live each day in a way that blesses God and those around us.

ENDNOTES

[1] Ronald F. Youngblood, *Unlock the Bible: Keys to Discovering The People and Places* (Nashville, TN: Thomas Nelson Publishers, 2011), 404.

[2] *ESV Study Bible*, (Crossway, Wheaton, IL.).1753.

[3] Ronald F. Youngblood, *Unlock the Bible: Keys to Discovering The People and Places* (Nashville, TN: Thomas Nelson Publishers, 2011), 408.

[4] *ESV Study Bible*, (Crossway, Wheaton, IL.).1753.

[5] Adapted from *The Quest Study Bible*, 1360.

[6] Ronald F. Youngblood, *Unlock the Bible: Keys to Discovering The People and Places* (Nashville, TN: Thomas Nelson Publishers, 2011), 124.

[7] Henry H. Halley, *Halley's Bible Handbook (Deluxe Edition)* (Grand Rapids, MI: Zondervan, 2000, 2007), 442.

[8] Bing online dictionary

[9] David Brow, A.R. Fausset and Robert Jamieson, *Critical Commentary and Explanatory on the Whole Bible* (Logosbible.com, 2011)

[10] Bing online dictionary

[11] Ibid.

[12] *The Quest Study Bible* (Grand Rapids, MI: Zondervan, 2003), 1363.

[13] Zodhiates & Baker, Hebrew – Greek *Key Word Study Bible* (La Habra, CA: AMG Publishers), 1242.

[14] *ESV Study Bible*, (Crossway, Wheaton, IL.).2478.

[15] David Brow, A.R. Fausset and Robert Jamieson, *Critical Commentary and Explanatory on the Whole Bible* (Logosbible.com, 2011)

[16] *ESV Study Bible*, (Crossway, Wheaton, IL.).1757.

[17] Ibid.

[18] *Bible Study Magazine*, Color Code, Eli T. Evans, July/August 2012, pg. 30.

[19] *ESV Study Bible*, (Crossway, Wheaton, IL.).1758

[20] David Brow, A.R. Fausset and Robert Jamieson, *Critical Commentary and Explanatory on the Whole Bible* (Logosbible.com, 2011), Chapter 6

[21] Ibid.

[22] *ESV Study Bible*, (Crossway, Wheaton, IL.).1759.

[23] Ibid.

[24] Bing online dictionary

[25] Ibid.

[26] David Brow, A.R. Fausset and Robert Jamieson, *Critical Commentary and Explanatory on the Whole Bible* (Logosbible.com, 2011), Chapter 6

[27] Ibid.

[28] Taken from a post written from Billy Graham, www.myhopewithbillygraham.org and posted on flashtrafficblog.wordpress.com

[29] *The Quest Study Bible* (Grand Rapids, MI: Zondervan, 2003), 1366.

[30] Ibid.

[31] David Brow, A.R. Fausset and Robert Jamieson, *Critical Commentary and Explanatory on the Whole Bible* (Logosbible.com, 2011), Chapter 8.

[32] http://www.chabad.org/library/article_cdo/aid/4825/jewish/Gedaliah.htm

[33] David Brow, A.R. Fausset and Robert Jamieson, *Critical Commentary and Explanatory on the Whole Bible* (Logosbible.com, 2011)

[34] *The Quest Study Bible* (Grand Rapids, MI: Zondervan, 2003), 1836, 1840.

[35] www.freedictionary.com

[36] Ibid.

[37] *The Quest Study Bible* (Grand Rapids, MI: Zondervan, 2003), 1369.

[38] Vernon McGee, *Thru the Bible – Genesis through Revelation,* (Thomas Nelson, Nashville, TN, 1998), 14831.

[39] *ESV Study Bible*, (Crossway, Wheaton, IL.).1765.

[40] Vernon McGee, *Thru the Bible – Genesis through Revelation,* (Thomas Nelson, Nashville, TN, 1998), 14831.

[41] Ibid.

[42] Ibid.

[43] Ibid.

[44] Ibid.

[45] *ESV Study Bible*, (Crossway, Wheaton, IL.).1766.

[46] Vernon McGee, *Thru the Bible – Genesis through Revelation,* (Thomas Nelson, Nashville, TN, 1998), 14877.

[47] www.biblestudy.org/greattribulation

[48] Vernon McGee, *Thru the Bible – Genesis through Revelation,* (Thomas Nelson, Nashville, TN, 1998), 14885.

[49] Ibid.

[50] *Key Word Study Bible,* (AMG Publishers, Chattanooga, TN, 2008.). 3027.

[51] Vernon McGee, *Thru the Bible – Genesis through Revelation,* (Thomas Nelson, Nashville, TN, 1998), 14932.

[52] *ESV Study Bible*, (Crossway, Wheaton, IL.).1767.

[53] www.freedictionary.com

[54] *ESV Study Bible*, (Crossway, Wheaton, IL.).1768.

[55] Vernon McGee, *Thru the Bible – Genesis through Revelation,* (Thomas Nelson, Nashville, TN, 1998), 14976.